A SUSSEX CHILDHOOD

TONY WALES

𝕾.𝕭. 𝕻ublication

First published in 2001
by S B Publications
19 Grove Road, Seaford,
Sussex BN25 1TP
01323 893498

© 2001 Tony Wales

ISBN 1 85770 240 9

Drawings by Alan Major

Typeset by JEM Editorial
Printed and bound by
Tansleys the Printers
19 Broad Street, Seaford
Sussex BN25 1LS
01323 891019

*Cover picture: Raphael Tuck
postcard – A Skipping Match
Title page: 1930s birthday card*

Contents

INTRODUCTION

This is a book of memories, mainly joyful ones. I hope the days of your childhood were mostly pleasant, with lots of sunshine, long holidays, and a freedom from care and adult obligations.

Well, we know, if we are really honest, that it was not always quite like that. But it is most enjoyable to remember the good times, and to convince ourselves that today's world is much harder and harsher.

So here are the games, the toys, the sweets and the other happy memories of our (and sometimes our parents') childhood. However, we must not forget the other side of the coin, and as we move back in time to recollections passed on to us by older relatives, so some of the accounts take on reflections of the occasional grim reality of everyday life. But much that was undoubtedly harsh and unfriendly I have omitted; so here for a while let us remember mainly the good things of the past.

Without the memories of many good friends, this book could not have been written. Therefore to all those mentioned at the end – and many others whose names I have not recalled – I dedicate this little book. The memories are undoubtedly very selective, and I feel sure that many readers will have others of their own equally valid, so feel free to pass them on to me – and - perhaps one day a second book will come about. Meantime – happy recollections.

Tony Wales

APRIL FOOLS

The origins of April Fools' Day (April 1) are wrapped in the mists of time, as they say. Folklorists sometimes mention a possible link with Lud, a Celtic god of humour, who celebrated his festival in the spring. As a day when practical jokes may be played with relative impunity, it is well known around the world. In Scotland an April fool is referred to as a gowk – a cuckoo. A man who was married to a foolish woman was sometimes known as an April gentleman.

The practical jokes carried out (mainly by children) still go on, although not perhaps as widely as in less sophisticated times. Many are relatively harmless – 'Do you want a stamp?' On receiving an affirmative, the joker stamps on the victim's foot. Or there are simple catches such as 'I one a snail', followed by 'I two a snail' and so on until the first child reaches 'I seven a snail', whereupon the victim (if he hasn't heard it before) utters the memorable phrase, 'I eight a snail' Ugh!

In my young days children dreamed of very elaborate jokes (which were seldom actually carried out) such as sending their friends on impossible errands for such things as pigeon's milk, left-handed hammers, straight hooks, striped paint, strap oil and other fictional items which were also invoked for fooling apprentices.

Like many other folk customs, April fool jokes must be carried out before noon, or the joker can be met with the immortal phrase: 'Up the ladder and down the wall. You're the greatest fool of all.'

AUTOGRAPH ALBUMS

The collecting of autographs still goes on, although now it is mainly the famous who are sought out for their signatures. In my youth it was our adult relatives and our friends who were expected to provide clever or witty entries for our autograph albums, and no doubt many of them had the snappy little rhyme or quotation stored readily at the back of their minds, so that they were not at a loss when the little book was thrust at them.

Here are a few typical examples:

> *When you are washing at the tub,*
> *Think of me with every rub.*
> *If the water be ever so hot,*
> *Lather away and forget me not.*

Many of the rhymes had as their main thrust the thought that the contributor should not be forgotten.

> ******* is my name,*
> *England is my nation.*
> *Sussex is my dwelling place,*

God is my salvation.
And when I'm dead and in my grave,
And all my bones are rotten.
This little book will tell my name,
When I am quite forgotten.

But enough of such serious thoughts, for many of the entries were in a much more humorous vein:

'Tis hard to part from loved ones,
To see them again we hope.
But 'tis harder to find the towel,
When your eyes are full of soap.

Of all the sad surprises,
There's nothing to compare,
With the treading in the darkness,
On a step that isn't there.

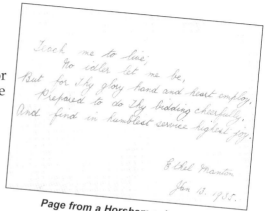

Page from a Horsham schoolgirl's autograph book of the 1930s

Sometimes the entries were decidedly unsuitable for young minds.

A camel can go without drink,
And work for a month without shirking.

6

But oft' when a man gets the hump,
   He'll drink for a month without working.

The next one could be amended to include the name of whatever town you called home.

   I dreamed that I died and to heaven did go,
   Where do you come from they wanted to know,
   Horsham I said, and didn't they stare.
   'Step right inside, you're the first one from there.'

A famous make of medicinal pills usually featured in collections such as this:

   Hark the Herald Angels Sing,
   Beecham's pills are a very good thing.
   Peace on earth and mercy mild,
   Two for an adult, one for a child.

But then Uncle Fred was always a very bad influence on his young nephews and nieces! By the end of the book, someone will be sure to have written:

   By hook or by crook, I'll be last in this book.

But there was usually just space enough for someone else to cap it with:

You're done.

A variation on the written contributions was a halfpenny stamp stuck in the middle of the page, with the accompanying message:

By gum – it's stuck.

or perhaps

I'm all stuck up.

It was all so very simple and unsophisticated – surely a million light years away from computers and mobile phones.

BIRDS' EGGS

Before more enlightened views on the natural world had become second nature – particularly in the minds of the younger members of the community – collecting birds' eggs was a very common pastime, especially where the boys were concerned. Sometimes great ingenuity was employed to find the scarcer eggs, and some collections were incredibly large. Eggs could be carried inside the large type of cap often worn by country lads. The enemy (whoever they happened to be at the time) could then land a quick blow with a well aimed fist on the cap, and the sticky result may be imagined.

The collecting of bird's eggs was believed by some to bring bad luck, although this seemed to have little effect on the popularity of the pastime. This applied particularly to robins' eggs. It was also believed that if you persisted in taking robins' eggs, then your fingers would grow crooked. Throwing eggshells on the fire would stop the hens from laying, it was thought, and you should always break the eggshell after eating an egg, otherwise the Devil (or sometimes it was the fairies) would use it for a boat. However, eggshells were not always broken, as sometimes great ingenuity was employed in decorating them, especially at Easter.

BIRD SCARERS

The country lads employed as bird scarers had one of the most miserable and least sought-after jobs on the farm, in the days when quite young boys were employed as soon as they could escape from the (usually) disliked schoolroom.

Perhaps on a fine sunny day it was not so bad, but to be stuck alone in the middle of a large field, for hours, on a cold and windy day, must have been boring and depressing in the extreme. Perhaps to ease the monotony just a little, some of these country lads used bird-scaring rhymes or songs. This was the best known one:

Shoo all up; shoo all up;
You eat my Master's corn up,
He has but liddle,
An' that's in the middle,
Shoo all up; shoo all up.

There was also a slightly more attractive rhyme:

We've ploughed the land,
We've sowed the seed,
We've made all neat and gay.
So take a bit and leave a bit.

So take a bit and leave a bit.
Away birds, away.

Writing in the *West Sussex Gazette* in 1979 a reader, Mr Pollard, told how his father left school in about 1880 to work on a farm. His job was bird-scaring, and given a pair of clappers he was left to sing:

Shoo all away. Shoo all away.
And don't come back no more today.
For if you do, I'll up with me clappers,
And knock you all backards.
Shoo all away. Shoo all away.

CATAPULTS

As any schoolboy in the past (and many adults) would tell you, the simple catapult was one of the most unobtrusive yet effective weapons ever devised. Now seen but seldom, it was once very popular with young marksmen, who often carried their skill into adulthood.

Any hardwood would provide the basic material, although yew or hazel were particularly favoured. Square elastic was essential – the round sort just would not do. A tongue from an old shoe added a touch of class to the weapon. Good shots knew that it was essential to keep the elastic warm between shots, so the catapult was invariably carried in the pocket.

Adult enthusiasts would have started young, becoming very attached to their 'catty', realising how silent and efficient it was in the right hands One of these was George Attrill, the fine old countryman of Fittleworth, who would not have dreamed of parting from his favourite weapon, having kept the same one for more than forty years.

The folk singer Bob Copper recalled his father's catapult which hung on a nail in his workshop. On the shelf below was a tin of 'chats' (tiny marble-sized potatoes) which were used as ammunition.

Another old friend, Doris Hall of Ditchling, remembered how her father came home one night full of anger at the unknown thief who had helped himself to his newly-planted 'taters. The following morning her father hid in a group of fir trees, catapult at the ready, to see if the miscreant would re-appear. 'He did, and Father shot him with his catty and brought him home in triumph. Mother made him into a pie, as the thief was a rook.'

John Millais (son of the Victorian artist John Everett Millais) was once known by many schoolboys not only as an author and big game hunter, but also as a great exponent of the humble catapult – from the time when he was a scholar at Marlborough College. He was a dead shot and could hit the point of a pencil from a distance of fifteen yards. One of the uses he put the catapult to was in hitting small birds; he claimed to have shot more than 200 with his weapon – something which today would be viewed with a very different attitude. But in his times he became a hero to many schoolboys, who longed to acquire his skill with the deadly little weapon.

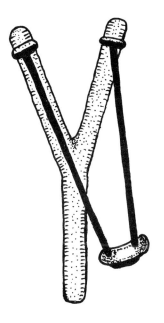

CHARADES

Charades was a party game much encouraged by adults, who apparently considered it sufficiently educational to deserve a strong degree of encouragement. A word is chosen by the group elected to provide the charade, and divided into syllables, which are then acted before the remaining audience – who are expected to guess the hidden word. Sometimes it worked well, but it depended largely on the acting skills of the participants – so a dull lot of actors could produce a very dull result. Perhaps my own memories of striving to produce a scintillating performance every time, and usually not succeeding, had something to do with my lack of enthusiasm.

Another somewhat similar game was known as *dumb crambo*, where a word or verse is chosen by one player. Another then chooses a second word which rhymes with it, and this must then be acted out in silence.

Girls in their white pinafore dresses at Graffham, early in the last century

CHEESE- EGG- AND ORANGE-ROLLING

These rituals crop up all around the country. Evidently the sight of something perfectly round just makes a child want to roll it. Two examples may be quoted from Sussex.

The Reverend WD Parish, in his *Dictionary of Sussex Dialect* (1875), speaks of cheese-rolling at Forest Row in 1894. He described it as: 'The ancient custom of rolling round cheeses down a steep hill in Kidbrooke Park, as part of a Summer treat for school children.'

In Brighton in 1883, on St Stephen's Day (December 26), it was the custom to bowl or throw oranges along the roads. The one whose fruit was hit by another forfeited it to the successful hitter.

Egg-rolling was also once popular with children at Easter time.

COLLECTING

Children (but in particular boys) have always been fond of making collections, often much to the disgust of their mothers, who despaired of keeping a boy's bedroom clean when it was adorned with things such as smelly dead birds and huge chunks of unidentified rock. I remember how in my own boyhood I delighted in the collection of curiosities which I had inherited from my father (which made the disposal of certain items difficult for my mother). There were two small stuffed crocodiles, an ostrich egg, a cross made from the Rock of Gibraltar, a stuffed baby chick, the skeleton of a rat which had managed to incinerate itself in someone's kitchen copper, plus lots of smaller items such as South-Sea island necklaces, old coins and unidentified seeds. My own additions to this motley collection must have worried my mother even more, as soon the collection threatened to take over my small bedroom. However, the crocodiles did wonders for my street-cred with my schoolfriends.

Many schoolboy collections must have been based on the wonderful (or terrible, whichever view you took) Museum of Curiosities amassed by Walter Potter at Bramber in 186l. The son of a local innkeeper, Potter spent his early years at home, developing a great interest in taxidermy. His first major work in this field was The Death and Burial of Cock Robin, which consisted of a showcase of no less than ninety-eight little stuffed birds. When exhibited at his father's inn, it attracted so much attention that he was given several commissions for more taxidermy work. This was at the time when stuffed animals in glass cases were very fashionable.

The House that Jack Built, one of the exhibits at Potter's Museum in Bramber

Other major tableaux which he executed for inclusion in his own collection included The House that Jack Built, The Kittens' Tea Party and The Upper Ten and The Lower Five. In every case small or baby animals were stuffed and put into human situations.

The philosophy of this concept is very much at variance with present day ideas, but as the work was done so long ago we can but wonder at the skill that it represented. I was taken as a child to see Potter's museum at Bramber. Walter died in 1918 but the museum had been carried on by his daughter and grandson and many items had been added over the years, so it contained not merely stuffed animals, but all kinds of weird and wonderful curiosities. In a present-day museum many would be completely out of place, but to a small boy at that period it was a little bit of heaven.

The museum at Bramber closed in 1972 and the collection moved to Brighton, near to the Palace Pier, and then to Arundel High Street. I viewed it here once again, but with older years the fascination had abated somewhat. It was still curious right enough, but also less acceptable to some visitors. Now it still charms (or puzzles) as a holiday attraction in the West Country.

Display cases at Potter's museum in Bramber

19

COMICS

Perhaps we should give them the more widely-used name of 'penny dreadfuls' which, rather than a term of derision, was looked upon by those who enjoyed them as almost a mark of approval.

Weekly comic books first made their appearance in Victorian days, and were very much a boys' thing. Adults, and especially school-teachers, viewed them with distaste, believing that they glorified crime. This attitude only added to their attraction, and the sense of danger experienced in smuggling copies of the forbidden books into school spiced up the monotony of daily life.

The comics introduced their readers to a dazzling array of characters – some of them genuine folk heroes – Rob Roy, Sweeny Todd, Deadwood Dick, Buffalo Bill, Charles Peace; boys loved them all, whether they were goodies or baddies.

Comic Cuts was probably the first of the periodicals, and still possibly the most famous. The first edition in 1890 was said to have sold out within a few hours, and was quickly followed by several spin-offs, such as the almost equally-famous *Chips*, and later slightly more respectable titles such as *Tiger Tim's Weekly, Chick's Own, Sunbeam, Rainbow* and *Tiny Tots*, all leading up to the modern names such as *Dandy, Beano, Wham* (and not forgetting in 1936, *Micky Mouse Weekly*).

What images these names evoke even in adulthood, and such bliss for just one penny (although later double this amount).

The more we enjoyed them, the more did authority in cap and gown detest them. I feel sure that my own schoolmaster positively relished the sight of one of the offending periodicals peeping from the top of a schoolboy's pocket, so that he could seize it and rip it to shreds. One day, when he attempted to treat what he believed was one of the detested comics in my possession in the normal manner, I was able to stop him by protesting that it was in fact a magazine published by a religious body in Ireland, with the title *Our Boys*. Admittedly it had the appearance of a boy's comic book, but he couldn't argue with the contents – so for almost the only time in my boyhood I felt I had scored a genuine point against authority.

Male readers will know that I have only scratched the surface of a delightful subject, but perhaps a few of the names mentioned will have conjured up images of bygone bliss.

Children enjoying the countryside at Gog View, Petworth, c1900

CONKERS

I am not sure who first picked up a conker and started playing with it, but whoever it was had a definite success on his or her hands. Most readers will know how to play conkers, and if they are grown-ups will suffer a tinge of regret that it is not used more generally as an adult game. Conkers are such attractive little objects that it is difficult to avoid the temptation to bend down and pick them up – even if you cannot find a suitable child to donate them to.

As with many old games, conkers has its own language. A *cheese-cutter* is a conker with a flat edge. *Strings* is the call when the strings holding the conkers become knotted together. When a player's conker falls to the ground without breaking, his opponent may call out *stampsies* and then stamp on it. However, this can be prevented by the first player calling out *no-stampsies*. *Round the world* is when one conker splits right round, and *skin trouble* is when there are cracks in the skin of the conker. *Death cracks* means that the conker is cracked and damaged.

Old hands at the game will have first baked their conkers in a brick oven to harden them. The holes will have been drilled with a hot knitting needle to avoid splitting. A bootlace is the most common item with which to suspend the conker.

In some places adults *do* play the game, and championships are held based on local pubs. Boredom has to be avoided, and one pub had the simple rule – 'An unnatural conclusion will be found for games lasting too long'.

In 1980 there was a serious dispute at Yapton over the rightful owner of a conker tree, which it was said had been used for many years by the local children.

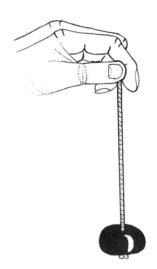

CYCLING

The cycling craze took hold in the late 1800s and early 1900s, as the modern style of cycle evolved. Children, when they could find an adult to provide the machine, loved them, and even young women – who were forced to weigh their long skirts down with lead weights – were captivated by the opportunity to travel distances previously only dreamed about.

The new asphalt roads helped too, and Cecil Cramp told me that his parents, as youngsters, took their cycles from Horsham to Handcross, just for the joy of riding up and down a hundred-yard stretch of the newly-surfaced main road when they arrived.

Sometimes the cycles were very much bone-shakers, made up with all sorts of odd parts and held together with string. Jean Sunderland told me that her father, when a boy, set out in the early 1900s to cycle to Brighton with another lad. The outing came to a sudden stop when, halfway up Clayton Hill, her father's bike broke clean in half. She never found out how they got back home. Ron Muggeridge told how, when returning from a trip to Five Oaks, he had five punctures. He and his mates took turns pumping up the tyres, and riding like mad before the tyres went down again. Some bikes had so many odd parts that the rider ended up with virtually a different machine from the one originally owned. The taunt in those days was:

Old iron never rusts.
Cushion tyres never bust.

DANCING BEARS

These unfortunate animals, mainly from Poland, were fairly common on Sussex country roads well into the twentieth century – and naturally children loved them, or at least little boys did; girls were less sure.

The bears were secured by chains and had been taught to dance on their hind legs, holding a pole in their forepaws. A trumpet or bugle was often used by the keeper to herald the bears' arrival. The task of making the animals perform must have been difficult at times as bears are not the easiest beasts to train. A correspondent in the *West Sussex Gazette* recalled one Sunday morning, about 1892, on the Warningcamp Road: 'My father and I saw four or five bears, including one very large one, taking their Sabbath rest against a high overgrown hedge. The trainers had apparently met at a quiet spot to spend the day together.'

Although most children looked forward to the bears' arrival, they were not always popular, and women were known to offer coppers to persuade them to move on to the next street. Sometimes elderly women were scared, and locked themselves indoors until the bears had moved on. One man allowed the bear-keeper and his charge to stay the night in an outhouse, much to the consternation of his wife and family, who spent their night in fear and trembling.

But others viewed them differently. Ethel Powel of Portslade told me: 'In the 1950s a great treat was the dancing bears – brought round the streets by their Italian masters.

The great brown things, each with a collar and chain round its neck, would lumber along the streets. Then one of the swarthy smiling men, with their flashing white teeth and gold earrings, would start playing an accordion. The bears would rise on their hind legs and dance solemnly round, to our great delight. The men usually had a tiny monkey as well, and they would come round with a tin cup for our pennies. Many times I was scolded for following the bears.'

Signor B Volpé and his bear Mishka,
of the Royal Italian Circus

DIABLOS

Very much as hula hoops and yo-yos became nine-day wonders in later years, so the devil-on-two-sticks, or diablo, caught the imagination of the juvenile section of the population in the early part of the last century.

It was described to me by Mrs H Goddard of Hurstpierpoint as: 'Like a cotton reel with grooves in the centre, held on a length of string which was joined to two sticks, held in the two hands.' The diablo was worked up and down, the young operator tossing it into the air and then catching it on the string. Apparently experts were able to perform all kinds of tricks, watched by their less adept friends. The diablo passed out of fashion like so many other juvenile crazes, and has not been revived – so far!

DOLLS AND DOLLS' HOUSES

Many of the things described in these pages belonged almost exclusively to the world of the boy – but dolls and dolls' houses have always been exclusively a girls' thing.

Dolls houses could be most elaborate and expensive, and some of these from the classic period of such treasures may be viewed, and wondered at, if you visit one of the fascinating toy museums. Sadly such toys were out of the reach of the average Sussex country child, who had to be content with something more basic, contrived by a father or older brother. An orange box, which provided a two-storey house, was the most popular item from which to fashion the finished article – being both cheap and easy to obtain. With a downstairs kitchen and an upstairs bedroom, this would have been very familiar to many of the children who played with such toys. A piece of material as a curtain across the front of the box was all that was required to keep the two rooms hidden when not being played with.

Dolls to inhabit the house could be made from dolly (clothes) pegs, with the heads and bodies suitable adorned with dresses and bonnets. But dolls were also made out of all sorts of other materials – items from the hedgerows or merely paper.

Paper was probably the most popular material for making dolls and other toys. Strings of paper dolls were easily cut out – and then there were the innumerable paper mats and doyleys fashioned from folded paper. I have often wondered what nineteenth century mothers did with all those paper mats given them by their industrious children.

A birthday postcard from the 1930s

EMPIRE DAY

Queen Victoria's birthday (May 24) – Empire Day – was once a most popular day in the schoolchild's year. It had taken the place of May Day (May 1), which tended to become less significant as the twentieth century advanced.

My own memories included parading with the Union Flag, having first persuaded the teacher that I was the most deserving candidate for the honour of carrying the flag. Later we were treated to a lecture on the importance of the Empire, and how sensible it was that the British ruled so much of the world.

Other schools seemed to have made even more of the event, usually ending their ceremonies with the welcome declaration of a half day's holiday. Bill Crouch told me that his two most significant days as a youngster in Lewes were Bonfire Night and Empire Day. For the latter they would go to school dressed in white, and then proceed with their flags to the Dripping Pan (the football ground). There they had a good sing-song and were then given the rest of the day off.

At Angmering in the 1930s the schoolchildren danced from the village hall up the hill to a field, where they danced round the Maypole. The girls wore head-dresses of real flowers (here we can see a throwback to the earlier May Day ceremonies).

In some schools one girl was dressed as Britannia, and others wore varied costumes of the Empire. But, almost always, the ceremonies ended with the popular permission for a half-day's holiday.

John Payne of Horsham wrote this letter to his sons, re-living the wonders of Empire

Popular patriotism – a celebration of Empire Day early in the twentieth century

Day in his youth. 'After the usual parade and flag waving, the children sang at the top of their voices:

We have come to school this morning,
'tis the 24th of May.
And we join in celebration,
On this our Empire Day.

The headmaster then made the anticipated declaration of a half-day's holiday, accompanied by cheers.'

John thinks that it was probably the beginning of the Second World War that put an end to these joyful days (or was it something to do with us having lost an empire?).

FAG CARDS

Yes, certainly 'fag cards' rather than cigarette cards, as that is how they were always known in my own childhood. I first remember them as something which my father handed out to me after he returned home with his weekly allowance of cigarettes. Then he changed his make of smokes, switching to Kensitas, which was including beautiful silk cards in the packets – and which he decided to keep for himself. Even so there were always fag cards around, being swapped and played with.

The cigarette companies took them very seriously, bringing out sets of fifty different designs ranging from film stars to racing cars. Albums to keep the cards were also available, and there was quite an educational aspect to the whole thing. But somehow we didn't think of them in that way; we used them as a sort of coinage (four cards equalled one farthing in my particular group) and they were always in demand for games.

Flick cards was the most popular way to use cards, with an eighteen inch square chalked on the pavement and the cards being flicked into this. Another variant was for cards to be flicked towards a wall. If one fell on top of yours, then you lost it. A further use for a card was to fix it on a cycle, in such a way that it made a very satisfying whirring sound as the front wheel went round.

FAIRS

Children have always loved fairs, and used to wait with tremendous anticipation for the traditional dates to come round, when they knew that the gaily-painted waggons would arrive without fail. Every town and many villages had their particular dates, and these were often used by adults to remind them of the best times to plant certain vegetables. Ebernoe Fair was when the locals planted their spring cabbages; Petworth was the time to plant broad beans, and Crawley, runner beans. Another saying relating to Crawley Fair was that it always rained on that particular day. But that didn't stop the Crawley youngsters from enjoying their favourite day of the year. This was how a broadsheet, sold at one Crawley Fair, celebrated the occasion:

> *The Annual Fair on the 8th of May.*
> *Was larger than has been for many a day.*
> *The stock in the field fetched a good price.*
> *The morning was wet, and then cleared off nice.*
> *There were several prime horses, some entire.*
> *The rain in the morning made the field in a mire.*
> *A very few pigs, a pen or two of sheep.*
> *But nothing in the field was sold very cheap.*
> *From the middle Square, down to The Sun.*
> *There was plenty of amusement for old and for young.*

A steam merry-go-round at the September Sheep Fair in Lewes, c1981

A good lot of horses by The George in the town.
Which were as usual galloped to fetch another pound.
There was Hoop-la and Darts, and Swings on the Green.
And Photographs Taken near the pavement was seen.
In the White Hart field there was plenty going on.
Two excellent Roundabouts belonging to Bond.
A number of Swings, and Cocoa-nut Shying.
Which were hard to be got with a lot of trying.
Hoop-la and Darts, and Throwing of Rings.
Shooting at Bottles, and other things.
In Penfolds Meadow, near to The Sun.
Was another Roundabout, a very good one.
No Trying of strength with Mallet or Bittle.
But other Side Shows belonging to Whittle.
As you entered the town in the Middle Square.
Two or three Cheap Jacks were very busy there.
The police were on duty, but things seemed quiet.
There was no drunken case, no fighting or riot.
Next day being Sunday, many cleared off spoon.
Some went home late by the light of the moon.

As can be seen, the old-time fairs were a mixture of animals and amusements. Children enjoyed it all, especially the noise and bustle which was so different from normal humdrum life.

Later in life, many older Sussex folk could conjure up happy memories of their youth when the fair arrived with its colour and gay music. At Adversane Fair you were warned not to eat pork until the great day. In 1984 Mr E Carley recalled how 'Old Mr Smith', always wearing his black bowler hat, would preside over the proceedings, with pork being roasted in a booth. The festivities usually ended with fights, and Sergeant Trott had to be fetched from Horsham to sort things out.

At Horsham Fair on the Carfax, (where the sounds and smells must have sorely tried the residents of the surrounding houses) the Fat Woman challenged anyone to span her calf with two hands – the prize being a bottle of wine. The children looked on in amazement at otherwise staid grown-ups behaving in such a fashion – although no-one ever succeeded in winning the wine. After one Horsham fair gypsies removed the Bull Ring, which was sited on the Carfax, and when its loss was discovered a party of irate locals set out to chase the thieves and bring back the town's property.

Sussex fairs were once famous for the sale of gingerbread which was much prized by youngsters and adults alike – more on this subject further on.

FLOWERS

Wild flowers grew in abundance around the early years of the twentieth century, and appeared to be so plentiful that no matter how many bunches were picked, the supply would never come to an end. May Day was especially noted for its use of wild blooms, and schools complained about the absent scholars, prior to May 1, who spent time in the fields gathering flowers instead of sitting at their desks. It was the girls who

Girls primrosing on the Downs near Brighton, c1936; note the stick to which bunches were tied for carrying them home

seemed to enjoy flowers the most, although even the boys joined in to some extent – picking the blooms which appeared to be never-ending. A common sight was of children on their cycles returning from lanes and fields, laden with bunches of bluebells and daffodils. Gypsies picked them too, and no-one seemed to mind, even when they brought them into the towns to sell in the streets.

Many happy hours were spent in the fields utilising the wild flowers in simple games – these being particularly beloved by the girls. For instance making daisy chains, for which you needed flowers with long stalks and big blooms. Buttercups held under the chin would answer the question – 'Do you like butter?' – and dandelions at the seed stage were ideal for checking on the correct time.

Early nineteenth century George Wood photograph of girls gathering flowers

GO-KARTS

Go-karting was most definitely a boys' activity, and the rougher element at that. My parents would have been shocked at any suggestion that I should own such a contrivance; in fact in the roads where I lived, these home-made vehicles were seldom seen. What they did not know was that as I travelled a few miles to school in a nearby village each day, I was well aware of both the simple and sometimes elaborate carts which were used not far from the school. These were made from wooden boxes and other scrap material, often I suspected with the connivance of a helpful father. The ones which had swivelling front wheels, so that by means of a loop of rope the cart could be steered, were most desirable. The owner sat in the cart, which had as its motive power another boy (usually younger) who was expected to push at the back. The carts were used on the pavements, so adults seeing them coming would quickly step into the road to avoid a mishap. As I well recall there was much rivalry between gangs with their carts, and the prestige of actually owning one was very great.

Boys will be boys, seen here with their own transport, outside Kipling's house at Rottingdean

42

GROTTOS

Oyster shell grottos were made by children in Brighton streets up to around the 1860s, on July 25 (St James's Day). The emblem of St James is a scallop shell, so it was suggested that the grottos originally commemorated the pilgrimages which were made to the shrine of the saint.

The rhyme which accompanied the grottos went like this:

Please to remember the Grotto.
Its only once a year.
Father's gone to sea.
Mother's gone to fetch him back.
So please remember me.

Similar grottos were also noted in London in more recent times.

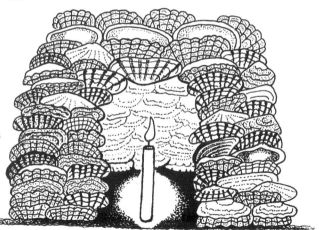

HOBBY HORSES AND ROCKING HORSES

The hobby horse has a rich history and even today remains an essential part of our English folk tradition. From the thirteenth century we learn that 'The Hobby Horse doth hither prance, Maid Marian and the Morris Dance'. Present day morris dancers are familiar with the hobby horse and in some places it plays an important role in annual customs associated with spring fertility rites. In imitation of adults and their 'horse-play', children have also had their own hobby horses – often simply made from a broom handle and a stuffed horse's head.

It was said that a home with a Rolls Royce car almost always had a rocking horse for its children. It was certainly not a poor child's plaything. My first introduction to a rocking horse was when I was taken to stay with my cousin. Her parents appeared rich by my own parents' standards and the thing that set them apart most particularly was the huge rocking horse kept on the landing at the top of the stairs.

HOOPS

My mother always said that her hoop was as important to her when she was young as a cycle would have been (if she could have afforded such a luxury). She tried to take it wherever she went, and could recall bowling it for miles along the country lanes.

The boys' hoops were of iron, and made a grand noise as they trundled along the bumpy roads. The girls' hoops were wooden, lighter but still quite large, sometimes bigger than the girls themselves. Winter was the time for hoops, and running alongside them must have helped the circulation considerably during the cold winter months.

The hoops were driven by a piece of metal with a round handle. This was known as a skidder, skiddaw skeller, skeeler, skimmer or some other similar name – always beginning with s. Often the village from which you came determined the particular name used. These essential items were made by obliging blacksmiths, and cost about twopence. Sometimes a daring child would sport a cotton reel, which revolved, fixed to the end of the stick as a bit of sophistication.

When an iron hoop snapped due to being bounced too hard, it would mean another visit to the

Let children play their merry game,
Strangers to strife,
God keep them safe from sin and shame
In after life.

blacksmith, who would charge a halfpenny to weld the two ends together.

So well-established as a child's shadow was the hoop, that some schools provided iron hooks on the outside walls for hanging them while the owners were at lessons.

Sometimes gangs of boys with their big iron hoops would charge each other from opposite ends of the street, attempting to knock over as many of each other's hoops (and their owners) as possible.

As a variant to a hoop, or perhaps if a child could not afford one, a boot-blacking tin lid might have to suffice. This would have a hole through the centre, and could be made to run alongside the owner if a piece of string were passed through the hole with a knot to hold it in place.

A coloured, embossed postcard from 1907, bearing the rhyme: 'Let children play their merry game, Strangers to strife, God keep them safe from sin and shame, In after life'

HOPSCOTCH

Even today it is not unusual to see hopscotch squares marked on pavements or school playgrounds, either in chalk or permanently painted. Children still take great delight in hopping from square to square to move a flat stone. Mrs M Moran of Bognor remembered playing this in the early 1920s under the name *peevers*. Sometimes buttons were used to play a version of hopscotch. In fact buttons were often in great demand, both as a sort of juvenile currency, and for playing different games. It was not unknown for buttons to be cut off coats hanging in the school porch, to the owners' consternation.

KNUCKLE-BONES

Also known as *jacks, fives, dabs* or *dibs*. This is a game of great age – to be seen on Greek vases, and mentioned in Russian historical records. It was played originally with the bones of sheep; later cubes of clay were used, and in more modern times nicely-moulded pieces of metal.

One of the advantages of these particular toys is that they can be played as a solo game or competitively with others. The object of the game is always to go through as many variations of play as possible. Usually five jacks are used, although my mother remembered playing with six, using ordinary stones of roughly equal size.

As can be seen, the possibilities are almost endless. The simplest action is to take all the jacks in the palm of the hand, throw them into the air and catch them on the back of the hand. More difficult is to hold all but one in the palm, throwing the remaining jack into the air, and removing one of the others before catching it. Another variation was to put one into your mouth, throw up the others, remove the one from your mouth, and still manage to catch the rest. Other possibilities included holding the stones between your fingers, or spread out on the ground. But in every case one or more of the little objects are thrown into the air, and some other action is undertaken before catching the ones thrown.

The game had its own vocabulary: *one-ers, two-ers, three-ers, trotting donkeys, fly catchers, ups and downs, dish clout* and much more.

MAGIC LANTERNS

These were an exciting bit of early technology in which coloured slides were projected onto a screen (usually an old sheet). The earliest lanterns had oil lamps but, later, more sophisticated lighting was introduced. Other improvements included slides with moving parts, so that people and objects could be seen to move while projected.

My own memory is of a fairly basic lantern, dating from my father's childhood. This had been converted to electric light. There was but a small supply of coloured slides, which I never tired of seeing. Most children's first sight of a magic lantern was when one was brought to the village school for a special treat.

Ethel Powell recalled the excitement in the family when her father acquired one of these exciting scientific marvels. He had only a few slides, so they watched them again and again. One of those she remembered particularly was of an Indian boy who had an elephant as a pet. In a subsequent slide a man was shown being cruel to the animal, and this was followed by another when the elephant squirted the man with water. There were also several slides which gave the words of popular hymns, such as *Dare to be a Daniel* and *Hold the Fort*, so these were considered to be very suitable for Sunday viewing.

Victorian magic lanterns are now eagerly sought-after by collectors. Don Attle of Angmering has been collecting examples for many years, and now gives shows to highly appreciative audiences, who find such wonderful examples of early technology completely enthralling.

Final slide from an Edwardian lantern show

50

MARBLES

Marble playing by adults in Sussex was taken very seriously, particularly in Lent, culminating in many games on Good Friday, which was often known as Marble Day. Not to be outdone by adults, children (especially the boys) also played marbles, but as with adults all marble- playing had to come to an end on Good Friday. If you attempted to play after that day, then

A game enjoyed by both young and old. Here champion marbler Sam Spooner plays with a young enthusiast

the cry went up *scrabbles* (or some other similar word) and you were then liable to have all your marbles confiscated by a bigger boy.

Marbles came in many types and sizes, from tiny pewits to the big tolly. If you ran short there was always the round glass ball in the neck of a ginger beer bottle, and many perfectly good bottles must have been sacrificed for the sake of the glass ball.

Children had many marble games, as my mother remembered. One of the most popular was when a big ring was chalked on the ground and was filled by marbles contributed by each player. Then each player, using his favourite tolly, took a turn to shoot, in order to get as many marbles as possible out of the ring. Any successfully removed were retained. Children's marbles were kept in cloth bags, probably made by obliging mothers.

Another game was *egg-in-hole*, originally played with eggs rather than marbles. Five holes in the ground were needed, and all one had to do was to get the marbles into the holes. The one who got most in won the rest of the marbles. Clare Chandler of Fletching remembered boys making holes in the ground for this game, using their caps to beat the dust out of the holes.

Another game was *throw block*, in which a block of wood, with letters burnt on it, was thrown into the air. According to the letter which landed uppermost, so marbles were won or lost.

A simple marble game recalled by my mother was known by several different names – *cannons*, *dobbers*, *gutter allys* or *follow after*. This consisted in rolling the marbles along the gutter, one aimed at another (useful for livening up the walk home from school, if you hadn't a hoop or top). A more complicated marble game was *kicks*, in which two players took turns to throw a marble against the side of a boot, in order to make it rebound as far as possible. The opponent then shot in the usual way, aiming to score a direct hit on the first marble. The skill was to throw against the boot in such a way as to present your opponent with a very difficult shot.

Much more organised was a game utilising a board with circular holes cut along the bottom of it, and with numbers marked above each aperture. The idea was to roll your marble through the hole with the highest number, thereby winning that number of marbles from your opponent. The higher numbers belonged to the smallest holes.

One more game was to mark a square on the ground, placing a marble at each corner and in the centre. The players used a tennis ball to knock the marbles out of the square in five throws, each taking turns. There must have been many more children's marble games, as names such as *bun-hole, holy-bang, nine-holes, boss-out, ho-go, ring-taw, lag, cob, long-taw* and *ante* have all been remembered.

Many children's marbles were very attractive, with a variety of colours and designs. Boys in particular valued their tollies and allys and tried very hard to keep them from thieving hands.

MAY DAY

Once a very important day in the life of a school child, until Empire Day, with a lot more official backing, took over in the early years of the last century. May Day had a slightly less than respectable history in English lore, but the Victorians cleaned it up and for several years it enjoyed great popularity with children who were encouraged to take part in May Day ceremonies, using flowers and the ever-popular Victorian version of the English maypole.

However, sometimes school attendances suffered, even before the day itself, when children went out collecting flowers for their May garlands. Some teachers encouraged the May Day celebrations, but others actively discouraged them, feeling that this was something over which they did not have complete control.

Where the May celebrations were still carried out, children enjoyed parading and taking part in competitions with their garlands or maypoles, which were flower-decorated poles. Clare Chandler of Fletching recalled:

The First of May is Maypole Day,
So please remember the Maypole.

We don't come here but once a year,
So please remember the Maypole.

The children then walked a mile to Sheffield Park for a contest on the lawn; the one judged to have the best garland was awarded a whole shilling.

One Sussex place where May garlands have not disappeared is Lewes, where Garland Day is still carried on with great enthusiasm. Here the rhyme is:

The First of May is Garland Day,
So please remember the Garland.
We don't come here but once a year,
So please remember the Garland.

Garland Day in Lewes

55

For Your BIRTHDAY.

To Carry my Wishes

My thoughts will fly to you To-day
To bring you every Joy,
I hope you'll have
a wonderful time
And be a Lucky boy.

T.798-2.

56

MECCANO AND TOY TRAINS

Boys, and even sometimes their sisters, loved mechanical things, particularly if they could be built with a modicum of skill. Meccano offered just that, with the added ability to take everything to pieces and rebuild it into something different. I inherited much of my Meccano from my father and the thought that I was using items which he had also played with as a boy added satisfaction to my natural enjoyment. Apart from the fact that my additional pieces were coloured, there seemed little to separate the new from the old. Thus many of my models were built using metal strips from a previous generation, joined to material bought just a week previously.

Toy trains have fascinated boys of all ages since real trains first appeared. Like the Meccano, much of my own network was secondhand, but in this case it came to me via my grandmother who somehow extracted it from the younger members of the family for whom she worked.

When my parents moved from a flat to a three-bedroom house they were initially unable to make use of the smallest bedroom. What a joy it was to lay out my train rails and be allowed to leave them intact from one day to the next. But what a blow when, after a few months, I was told in no uncertain terms that the room was to be furnished as a spare.

Now, many adults are not ashamed to admit to a passion for playing with trains, and miniature railways are likely to spring up in the most unlikely places.

OUTDOOR GAMES

Perhaps we should have a whole book devoted to outdoor games as there are so many. Some had particular seasons, while many others were popular all the year round. The more rowdy games belonged particularly to the boys, but there were also many that were played by both girls and boys.

One game which often crops up in people's memories is *British bulldog* (or *English bulldog*). Some will remember it as merely an excuse for the boys to pile on top of one another, but it was actually a little more complicated than that. The boys were divided into two teams, opposite each other in a single file. The leading boys in each file folded arms and hopped towards each other, attempting to knock their opponents off balance. The side with most members left standing at the end of the game was the winner.

A somewhat similar game was described to me under the name of *jocky wagtail*. In this one boy had his back to the wall, with the rest facing him. Then they bent down to make a line of backs, whilst their opponents had to run and jump on them, attempting to break the line.

Another game often recalled is *fox chase*. One child was elected to be the quarry and set off across country shouting *hulloa*. The others then followed, sometimes running for miles before they caught their fox.

Even more exciting was a game played after dark (parents may not have known about this). It was called *jack-o-light*, and required two boys with a lantern to set off, giving the rest five minutes' grace before they were followed. Then the gang would call

Ring a ring of roses, a pocketful of posies

on the quarries to show their light, which would result in a mad rush to reach them – although by then they might be much further away.

A crude version of cricket was known as *conjer* (or *fog*). The wickets were rings scratched on the ground, and the bats straight sticks. The conjer was a short piece of wood about four inches long, which took the place of a ball.

As Sussex roads became busier, so a rather dangerous game developed known as *last across*. A line of children would start to cross the road in front of one of the new-fangled motor cars, and the one who got across in the slowest time was the winner. If the vehicles were motor buses then the object was to touch both wheels on the way.

Some games were aimed at the children's usual enemies, the adults! *Tickle-the-spider* consisted of hanging a button on six inches of thread, attached by a pin to a window frame. A second thread was attached to the first, just above the button. This could then be jerked back and forth across the frame, causing the button to make a highly satisfactory tap on the window. This was similar to the ever popular *knocking-off ginger,* which was the basic prank of knocking on doors and running away. I give the name that seems to have been most widely used in Sussex – although there are, it appears, around sixty different names. There was also the classic *hot-penny*, or *penny on a string*, in which a penny was placed in the path of a trusting pedestrian.

A very old game, *kiss in the ring,* had a long history of popularity in Sussex – and not merely with children. Summer events often ended up with this game being played in a suitable tent, to the disgust of the more staid members of the community. When it began to die out, the *Brighton Herald* was pleased to report in 1897, *kiss in the ring* was indulged in by only a limited number and it was of a decidedly mild order.

Some playground games could be really rough. *Wild horses* had two boys with linked hands behind their backs, charging around and looking for others similarly linked. A charge was then made; no pulling up, just crash and one of the pairs disintegrated.

Dumps was a kind of 'it' with a tennis ball. All the players stood in a circle with one foot forward, and all toes touching. One player, without looking, dropped the ball in the centre, and whoever it hit tried to retaliate by punching the ball. This then carried on until only one player was unscathed, and he was the winner.

Mr SL Longhurst of Battle recalled a game popular about 1915-20. It was called *bully-rooten* and was played with spars, the hazel sticks used in thatching. Each player in turn raised a spar over his shoulder, and with a powerful swing sent it into the soft earth. The next player did the same, trying to uproot those of the previous players. Any spar uprooted was out, and the game continued until only one was left.

Cherry lobbing was a boys' game. The boys would collect, wash and dry as many cherry pips as possible. Then a decision was taken on how many 'up'. If, say, ten was agreed, then a rainwater pipe was chosen, and the ten pips were pushed up the pipe as far as they would go. When they rolled down again, the players would note which had rolled the furthest. This would be repeated by each boy, and the winner was the one who had contributed the pip which had travelled the longest distance.

Red Rover required one child to face a wall, with the others on the opposite side of the road. The first player called out the number of steps the others were allowed to reach him, but as soon as he turned round everyone had to stop. Anyone caught moving had to return to the start. The first one across became Red Rover next time.

These were just a few of the games once played, but there were many more, all typical of the ingenuity of children before the days of television and computer games.

PARTY GAMES

These were normally a little more organised and sedate than the outdoor games, as parties were generally under the firm control of a parent, aunt or teacher. A very quiet game was *family coach* in which every child represented one particular part of the coach, and had to get up and curtsey or bow when that part was mentioned in the story being told by the grown-up. Rather more riotous was a game remembered by George Belton called *sing, say or pay*, and it required all the family sitting round in a ring. As your turn came, you had to sing a song, tell a story or pay a forfeit. After your turn you could call on anyone you wished, and he or she, in turn, could elect someone else, or pass it back to you (sometimes it would go back and forth between two rivals for some time). George said you always tried to pick on someone who was lacking in ideas, just for devilment.

Winks was a party game recalled by Bill Creighton. This had half the group sitting in a circle of chairs, one of which was unoccupied. Behind every chair stood another player. The one behind the empty chair winked at another player, who had to make a dash for that chair. At the same time, his or her way was hindered as far as possible by the person standing behind that chair. A kiss was said to be the reward for success, so perhaps adults enjoyed this game rather more than children.

Poor Pussy was very much a children's game, with Puss kneeling in the middle of a circle. The player who was the cat approached a seated players and made suitable noises, while the sitter stroked Puss and crooned *poor pussy, poor pussy*. Puss meanwhile tried to make the sitting player laugh, and if successful, the two changed places.

Some games were considered particularly suitable for Sundays. One of these was *clocks* remembered by RH Charters, from around eighty years ago. A circle was drawn and divided into segments, each being numbered from one to twelve like a clock. Players had to recall and write down a line from the Bible for each number, such as *Jesus wept* or *God is love*. The others then had to find this in the Bible. I cannot imagine this being particularly popular with present-day youngsters.

Forfeits were very much a part of parties in the nineteenth and early twentieth centuries, both for children and, surprisingly, adults. In the case of the latter, the forfeit might be a penny, which when added up would provide beer for the company. Children's forfeits were more complicated, and could consist of almost anything from singing a song to deciphering a puzzle – such as show two bare legs. This for a sedate Victorian miss could be quite a worry, until she realised that a table without its normal covering could provide more than enough legs for her purpose.

A classic party game, usually played by adults, but enjoyed also by youngsters, was *up jenkins.* Two teams sat on opposite sides of a table, one side having a coin hidden in one person's hand. The other team had a captain, who gave the orders. The first order was *up jenkins*, and all the hands came up with clenched fists. Then followed *elephant gate openers* (opening and shutting hands very quickly), *creepy crawlies* (scrabbling about on the table), *butterflies* (waving of hands up and down), *lobster pots* (fingers dancing on the table) and the climax, *smashoms*, when all the hands came down with a crash. The point of all this activity was to discover who held the coin. The captain finally ordered all the hands to be withdrawn, except the one he thought was holding the money. If he was right, then the team with the prize handed it over to the other side.

PEEP SHOWS

These could be as elaborate or as simple as desired. The usual peep-show was made from a shoebox (or similar), with the lid replaced by tissue paper to allow light to penetrate. The scene inside was viewed by an aperture at one end, and consisted of several tableaux, each one complementing the one behind it. In a simple form these would be made by cardboard cut-outs, coloured by hand – the effectiveness depending on the owner's artistry and ingenuity. A thing of the past one would imagine, although in the early 1980s I came across a young man at a garden fête with several well-made peep-shows. He was charging a penny a peep – and getting it too.

Floral peep-shows were once called poppy shows in Sussex. Blossoms, leaves and grasses arranged in patterns on a piece of card, had glass laid over them, and were then viewed with evident delight.

PENNIES

Even new pennies are not of great interest to children today, in fact such low-value coins are often seen on the ground laying undisturbed. But it was not always so. Even as recently as the 1940s, pennies were valued for what they could purchase, and street beggars and musicians seldom expected to be rewarded with anything greater. I have a dim memory of mudlarks in some Sussex seaside town, scrabbling for pennies thrown to them as they waited in the mud beside a river bank. Elsie Vincent of Horsham told me that during the summer months, children would collect on the green at Horsham's Dog and Bacon and call out to the returning day-trippers in their charabancs: 'Throw out your rusty coppers.' This was immediately followed by a mad scramble, as the passengers obliged.

Sometimes children were expected to work a bit harder for their pennies. At Rye there is a tradition of the new mayor throwing hot pennies from the upper floor of the town hall. They are heated in an oven and about £20 is distributed in this fashion.

A somewhat similar tradition exists at Hastings, but here it is apples, nuts and oranges which are thrown from windows.

PUT AND TAKE

My mother's particular treasure was a small but heavy brass top-like object ,with numbers on each of its six flat sides. It was spun like a top, and when it stopped and fell sideways, the number uppermost was noted and used for different games, or as a game on its own. Nowadays we would use a dice, but this always seemed to me to be much more fun. I particularly remember one day that after playing with a much older boy, my mother's precious put-and-take was missing. Eventually, after a family council of war, it was decided that the boy in question had walked off with the little object. Following even more enquiries it was found that this was indeed the case, and the put-and-take was retrieved with the help of his mother, and all was well.

RAT AND SPARROW CLUBS

When money was scarce, activities which produced a little extra cash were always welcome. Among these were the rat and sparrow clubs which flourished in many Sussex villages – supported by both men and boys, who found it a very satisfying way of enjoying a bit of sport and making a few extra pennies.

The club was often run by the local farmer, although at Berwick it appears to have been much more a village activity, with the parson as president and chairman. The payment was sixpence per dozen for old sparrows and two shillings a dozen for old rats (young ones fetched rather less). There were also quarterly cash prizes for those who caught the greatest numbers. No member could qualify unless he had caught sixty sparrows and fifteen rats in the parish. Members caught smoking in stockyards while catching were disqualified for all prizes.

Mr F Barton told me of his memory of the club in Rushlake Green. Here the rate was one penny for a sparrow's head, and twopence for a rat's tale. Nets were used at night to catch the sparrows.

Len Reed, writing in *Slinfold Through Eighty Years*, recalled how the local club claimed to have accounted for 89,462 sparrows' eggs in ten years.

At Southwater three persons could catch fifty or sixty sparrows in one evening, and local boys were encouraged to collect sparrows' eggs. Sometimes the sparrows were plucked and made into pies.

Catsfield Sparrow and Rat Club was well organised with a treasurer and secretary, and a subscription of one shilling annually (surely more than most youngsters could have managed). Moreover any member not producing 100 heads or tails before March 1 was fined sixpence, so this must have been a very prosperous neighbourhood.

In many villages the clubs were part of the social life, and often the farmers would hold a supper at the start of the year to encourage the men and boys to assist them in keeping down what were seen as very great pests. Now agriculture has changed, and farmers no longer depend on the activities of such clubs to help them grow their crops But once it was very much a question of:

> *One for the rook, and one for the crow.*
> *One for the mouse, and one to sow.*

RHYMES

Another subject which requires a complete book. Children have always loved rhymes, and grown-ups usually encouraged them (unless the rhymes were rude) as it made many things easier to remember.

Here are just a few examples of Sussex children's rhymes relating to natural things:

The first butterfly you see
 Cut off its head across your knee.
 Bury the head beneath a stone,
 And lots of money you will own.

White horse, white horse,
 Bring me good luck.
 Blow three times,
 And never look back.

You then made a wish.

Pea pod hucks, twenty for a pin.
 If you do not like 'em,
 I'll take 'em back agin.

This must date from the times when a pin was given for change in certain shops.

Tell tale tit, your tongue shall be slit.
 And all the dogs on Chailey Green,
 Shall have a little bit.

You can substitute some other village.

Bishop Bishop Barnabee,
 Tell me when my wedding shall be.
 If it be tomorrow day,
 Open your wings and fly away.

A gift on the thumb is sure to come,

A gift on the finger is sure to linger.

This refers to white specks on fingernails.

> *Man to the mow,*
> *Boy to the sow,*
> *And maid to the cow.*

Probably considered sexist these days.

> *One leaf for fame,*
> *And one leaf for wealth,*
> *And one for a faithful lover.*
> *And one to bring you glorious health,*
> *Are all in a four leaf clover.*
> *Marry when the year is new,*
> *Joy and riches both to you.*
> *When February birds do mate,*
> *You may wed, nor dread your fate.*
> *Marry when March breezes blow,*
> *Joy and sorrow, both you'll know.*
> *Marry in April if you can.*
> *Joy for maiden and for man.*

> *Marry in the month of May,*
> *You will surely rue the day.*
> *Marry when June roses grow.*
> *Over land and sea you'll go.*
> *All who in July do wed.*
> *Must labour always for their bread.*
> *All who wed in August be,*
> *Many a change are sure to see.*
> *Marry in September's shine,*
> *Your living will be rich and fine.*
> *If in October you do marry,*
> *Love will come but riches tarry.*
> *If you wed in dull November,*
> *Only joy will come, remember.*
> *When December snows full fast.*
> *If you marry, love will last.*

RIDDLES

In the past almost as popular as rhymes, although nowadays a little out of fashion. Here are just a few that delighted children in past years.

What is a footless stocking, without a leg?
Nothing.

Open like barn door, shut up like a trap,
You can guess a thousand things,
And never think of that.
A pair of knee-length knickers with an opening at the back.

What key unlocks a man's tongue?
Whis-key.

Why can't you hang a man with a

On the beach at Seaford

Children playing outside Maresfield's church

wooden leg?
Because you need a rope.

As round as an apple, as deep as a cup.
And all the Kings horses can't pull it up.
A well.

Why did the bull rush?
Because he saw the cow slip.

Why did the cow slip?
Because she trod on a butter cup.

Two legs sat on three legs, with one leg upon
his lap. Along came four legs and ran away
with one leg. Up jumps two legs and throws
three legs at four legs. To make four legs
bring back one leg.

A Sussex classic this one. The answer is a
man sitting on a milking stool with a leg of
lamb on his lap. A dog steals the lamb and
the man throws the stool at it to make it
bring it back.

There are many more, but to conclude here is a riddle song learnt from my mother. I remember her singing it to me when I was quite young, and I always found it absolutely fascinating. She had learnt it from her mother and it had been taught to *her* by her father.

I've got three sisters across the sea,
Piri-iri-ig-dum, do-man-wee.
And very nice presents they all sent me,
Port-um, quart-um, peri-cum-pla-cum,
Piti-iri-ig-dum, do-man-wee.

The nonsense lines are repeated throughout the song.

They sent me a cherry without a stone,
They sent me a chicken without a bone.

They sent me a book that's never been read.
They sent me a blanket without a thread.

How can there be a cherry without a stone?
How can there be a chicken without a bone?
How can there be a book that's never been read?
How can there be a blanket without any thread?

Children playing at Riverdale St John's, Crowborough, early in the twentieth century

When the cherry's in the bud, it's without a stone.
When the chicken's in the egg, it's without a bone.
When the book's in the press, it's never been read.
When the blanket's on the sheep, it's without a thread.

I sang this song in a folk song concert in London, and was followed on the bill by an American folk singer who was absolutely delighted to be able to sing a song from his repertoire which, although to a different tune, and with the words arranged a little differently, was without any doubt the same song. A perfect example (entirely unplanned) of how English folk songs travelled to other English-speaking countries.

SAMPLERS, SEWING, KNITTING

These were pieces of needlework, usually (although not always) worked at home by girls. They were intended to show the young woman's skill as a needlewoman and also her command of her letters.

Grandmother's sampler, which was almost lost to the family

My paternal grandmother was responsible for a very fine sampler in 1879. In my memory it always graced a wall, originally in my grandparents' home, and later in my parents'. After I married, the sampler continued to reside on the wall at the top of the stairs in my father's and step-mother's home, until one day my father told me quite casually that he had sold it in order to buy a much-needed raincoat. My distress on hearing this was not passed on to him, as I felt it was entirely his decision to dispose of such an article – and he obviously had no idea that it meant a lot to me. However, my dear wife decided to take matters in hand. She visited the shopkeeper who had quite unwittingly bought the sampler, and negotiated to buy it back. This was effected (much to my father's later surprise) and it still graces an important bit of wall in my own home.

Now samplers command high prices and are much sought after by collectors. Usually they contain such phrases as – '...... *is my name, England is my nation. Sussex is my dwelling place, and Christ is my salvation* (compare this with similar rhymes found in autograph albums).

Other phrases have an even more definite religious theme. For instance, *Lord thy light and truth bestow. On a child of low degree. Grant me grace that I may know. Something of myself and thee.* This is on a sampler of 1830 and was seen in the Priests' House folk museum at West Hoathly several years ago. Another tells us: *Ann Weller is my name. And with my needle mark the same. And by this you all may see. What care my parents took of me* (this from 1841, in the same collection).

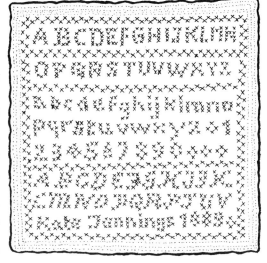

Girls were expected to master all the skills of a needlewoman while still children, such as learning to knit and crochet as well as sew. Woollen scarves, kettle holders, dish cloths and teapot mats were lovingly made and given as gifts for Christmas and birthdays. For the very young there was so-called French knitting, which produced satisfying, if rather useless, ropes and cords by means of a cotton reel and a few tin tacks.

SAND CASTLES AND PEBBLES

All these have always given great pleasure and satisfaction to children, and even at times, to their parents. Sand castle building has been a popular pastime at Sussex seaside resorts since our ancestors first discovered the attractions of the seaside, although it really came into its own in the late Victorian age.

Pebbles and shells were brought home in large numbers in Victorian and Edwardian days, and were then used to decorate fancy boxes, or were fashioned into animals or other little figures. Children have always been fascinated by the apparent sound of the sea, which can be heard when certain shells are held up to the ear.

In the 1800s oyster shells were used by children to construct grottos in the streets, when the cry was 'A penny for the grotto'.

Seaweed was also collected by children and taken home – much to many a mother's irritation. This was used to make pictures, or to hang outside the back door as a weather guide.

In 1835 Oliver Gates established a shop in Brighton selling pebbles and stones. Later his daughter published a little book, *Pebble Finding*, which named some of the many kinds of stones and pebbles to be discovered on Brighton beach. In this she said: 'One half of what are counted difficulties in this life have their root and growth in our constitutional laziness, and may be overcome with a little energy. We have all of us an eye for ripe cherries and red roses, why not for pebbles?'

Why not indeed, and in this little book we learn how children in Edwardian days found great pleasure in searching for the many different kinds of pebbles to be discovered on Brighton beach. However, the book concludes with the remark that Brighton as a haunt of the pebble-hunter is not what it was.

SCOOTERS

Scooters are once again enjoying a bout of popularity, even if the current metallic ones seem a little different from the mainly wooden models of past years.

In my childhood scooters were a sign of affluence. Go-carts and roller skates were fairly commonplace, but scooters meant that parents could afford to indulge their offspring when present-giving time came around. If those remarks betray a certain amount of jealousy, then that is probably the truth.

Half a century and more ago there was so little traffic in residential roads and on housing estates that it was safe for children to tear down hills and around the streets of their neighbourhood unsupervised.

SHADOW PLAYS

These were part of home-made entertainment in the early and middle years of the last century. All that was needed was a large white sheet hung up, with some form of illumination behind it. Children then used their ingenuity to act their own plays or sketches for the benefit of any audiences available.

Mrs M Lovely of Littlehampton told me of her memories of lighting up a sheet with candles or an oil lamp. A large horn gramophone was used to provide incidental music, and various love scenes, murders and melodramas were acted, providing the story had good visual impact.

SHRIMPING AND CRABBING

One of the special joys of a holiday by the sea was being allowed to behave in a completely different way from the rest of the year at home. For instance, one could dress much less formally, forsaking even shoes and socks. And the sand that persisted in remaining between one's toes, even when in bed at night, was to be welcomed as it contradicted all normal rules.

The first thing to be purchased at the start of a seaside holday was a shrimping net. Then there was the joy of finding pools left behind by the obliging sea – in which, if you were lucky, there would be baby crabs, shrimps and other maritime creatures, all waiting to be transferred to one's brightly-coloured toy bucket.

I cannot remember what happened to them at the end of the long summer's day, although I suppose they were returned to their watery home when all entreaties to be allowed to take them back to the boarding house fell on deaf adult ears.

SKIPPING AND SINGING GAMES

M any staid and respectable elderly ladies remember with great affection the simple singing games from their early playground days. Around fifty years ago I helped a newspaper to organise the collection of these rhymes, and my grandchildren tell me that some similar ones still survive. Here are some of the older ones:

1,2,3,4,5,6,7, All good children go the heaven.
Penny on the railway, twopence on the sea.
Threepence on the roundabout, out goes she.

I am a Girl Guide, dressed in blue.
These are the actions I must do.
Bend my knees, salute to the King.
Bow to the Queen, turn my back on the girl in green.
I am a Girl Guide dressed in yellow,
Shut my eyes and see my feller.
I am a Girl Guide dressed in black,
Went to work and got the sack.
Went to school, and got the cane.
Now I'm coming home again.

A Raphael Tuck postcard, Fun and Frolic, from the Oilette series, c1904

I am a Girl Guide dressed in red.
How many stairs to go to bed.
I am a Girl Guide dressed in green.
Shut my eyes and count sixteen.

Early in the morning, at eight oclock.
You should hear the postman knock.
In comes Mary knocking at the door.
How many letters on the floor.
1,2,3 etc.

Have a cigarette Sir, No Sir, Why Sir?
Cause I got a cold Sir, Where did you get your cold Sir?
Up the North Pole Sir. What you doing there Sir?
Catching Polar Bears Sir. How many did you catch Sir?
One Sir (up to six) and the last one caught me, Sir.

Who stole the key from the cooks canteen,
Was it you, number one?
Who, me?
Yes, You.
Couldnt be! Then who?

Continue with number two and so on and so on.

Rather older than the foregoing was:

Now you're married I wish you joy.
First a girl and then a boy,
Seven years now, and seven to come.
Take her, kiss her, and send her home.

Some games had historical backgrounds, such as Queen of Marlborough Towers noted in Rottingdean. This was played by the queen, her daughters and soldiers on one side, and two girls, as the enemy, on the other. The object of the game was to break the clasped hands of the enemy by sheer weight. The cry was: 'What is your complaint?' to which the singing reply was: 'We won't surrender to the Queen of the Marlborough Towers.' This game is found in different guises in many places.

Many games were firmly rooted in local lore. In his entertaining book *Alexandra Terrace*, A Longley quotes an East Worthing skipping rhyme:

Wally Wally Wallflower,
Growing up so high.
We're all ladies,
And we shall have to die.
Except Ena Kirton,
She's no relation.
She can go and turn her back,
To all the congregation.

Skipping, either with or without an accompanying rhyme, is a very old pastime, which once had definite magical connections. The last relic of ritual skipping in Sussex was the custom of children and adults skipping on Good Friday. This was once widely carried out at Brighton and in much of the surrounding area, but undoubtedly the Second World War had a lot to do with the passing away of this delightful ritual. Several attempts have been made in more recent years to revive Good Friday skipping in Sussex, and one can never be certain that it has completely died out, as it has a habit of popping up unexpectedly from time to time. In recent years the Knots of May women's morris team revived the custom and each year organise long-rope skipping outside the Rose Cottage pub at Alciston on Good Friday.

SQUIRREL HUNTING

This was an old custom known in Sussex as andring, skugging or just skug (at Newick they called it Saint Adring). It was carried out annually on November 30, St Andrew's Day.

Men and boys went in groups to the woods, armed with sticks – usually short pieces cut from broom handles, sometimes tipped at one end with metal. These were known as libbets, and were to throw at the unfortunate squirrels. It was noted until the 1870s, persisting longer in some places. At Mayfield it took place in 1903, but on Good Friday.

Writer Arthur Beckett wrote at length about a Sussex eccentric, James Hackman, who lived in the latter part of the eighteenth century. One year he sent out 100 invitations to the annual squirrel hunt. On the day he dressed in ancient armour and, attended by his squire, armed himself with firelock and bayonet. He then led a procession through the town and after the end of the sport presented everyone with an apple pie. He had caused 500 pies to be baked for the day, and the enjoyment of these was followed by a dinner at the local inn.

STAMP COLLECTING

Described as the king of hobbies (because George V was a keen collector) this quickly proved itself to be one of the most enduring and popular pastimes for boys (somehow girls never took it up to the same extent).

In the early days stamps were collected more as pretty bits of paper than as objects of any real value. They were threaded on strings (to make serpents) and pasted to make designs on tea trays and screens (here we pause to allow modern day philatelists to shudder, as they think of all those penny blacks and twopenny blues with holes through their middles).

But soon a more scientific approach came about, and with the advent of catalogues, and such tools as tweezers and watermark detectors, even the humble school boy prized his collection.

Like others I followed my father, when he collected specimen stamps given away with Black Cat cigarettes. He allowed me to have his duplicates, and soon I was the proud possessor of an album and a packet of stamp hinges. I badly wanted to go one better than my dad, and so I raided my money box and spent the huge sum of fourpence on a large Latvian stamp, which I was assured by the shopkeeper was a great rarity. Taking it to school, I impressed all my fellows with my valuable possession (the girls seemed less overwhelmed). Then horror, my valuable stamp disappeared. I reported the find to the headmaster, and the thief was discovered to be a boarder who was noted for

The Jubilee Stamp House at North Bersted

his liking of other boys' possessions. He was duly punished, and my rarity was restored to its honoured place in my album – although I was told not to bring such valuables to school in future.

My aunt, hearing of my interest in stamps, promised to take me to see the famous stamp house at The Rising Sun Inn, North Bersted, near Bognor. As this attraction flourished during Victoria's reign, I feel she was a little too late, but her intention was good. Richard Sharpe's unique Jubilee Stamp House opened during the latter part of the nineteenth century, and was described as being the most wonderful collection in the world. The stamps were stuck on the walls, the ceilings, and almost everything that would hold them. It was claimed that nearly a million were hung in festoons from wall to wall, giving the place a Christmassy appearance. Huge bundles of stamps, some containing as many as 60,000, were hung from the ceilings. A booklet was produced for sale to the visitors, of which it was claimed there had been 564,600 from the period when the exhibit had first been seen.

TADPOLES AND NEWTS

For children, both boys and girls, tadpoles, newts and efts have always held a tremendous fascination, coupled with a firm desire to take at least one of them home in the obligatory string-handled jam jar. Adults usually had quite different ideas, and always believed that the attractions of the local pond were best enjoyed in situ.

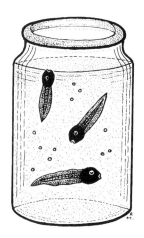

Pupils of Rudgwick School re-create the past, in 1980

TOPS

The top is an ancient toy, once very popular in the winter months. The boys had peg-tops which they set going by winding a string round the peg and then tossing the top down on the ground. Sometimes they would make a competitive game out of it, forming a circle of about ten feet with the competitors ranged around it. A top was set a-spinning, and the other players tried to knock it over with their own tops. There was an art in winding and tossing tops, and they could be tossed overhand or underhand (girls usually threw underhand). A hum was the indication of a top well thrown, and a peg top skilfully thrown would start humming while still airborne. Other types of tops were known as carrot, cabbage, mushroom, old ladies and window breakers.

The girls seem to go for tops made to spin with a whip, and an expert could keep one of these spinning along the pavement for the whole length of the street. Coloured paper stuck on top of the spinning top provided a pretty effect. Bootlaces were useful as whips for the tops.

Jim Laker of Three Bridges recalled how, as a boy, he played with other lads with their tops in the road between the school and a shop kept by an old lady who was noted for her meanness. When the school bell went, the boys ran into school, often leaving their string and even the tops themselves in the road. When they came out they would find their discarded string collected and wound up into halfpenny balls, and the tops scrubbed and offered as new in the window of the hard-fisted shop lady.

TOYS

Toys could be very simple or occasionally very elaborate, although it was the simple sort that most children of the past enjoyed. Of these a great many were home made, and it was quite amazing what a few pieces of wood and a little ingenuity could produce.

Bob Copper recalls key guns, which were made from a barrel type key, with a sawn off nail to fit into the barrel. The heads of three or four safety matches were crumbled and loaded into the barrel, and then the nail inserted. Held by a string, the contrivance was swung forcibly against a wall. Usually this produced a most impressive explosion, sometimes even splitting the key.

A little less dangerous was a tater-gun, or pea-shooter. This was usually made out of elder wood hollowed out, or a piece of metal tubing. It was loaded by pressing the muzzle into a potato, swede or mangold. The pellet was then ejected by pushing on a plunger.

A satisfactory explosion could be produced by partly filling a tin with carbide. You then added water, hammered the lid back on quickly and then retired to wait for the bang.

Ron Muggeridge, in his book *Warnham, A History* (1985), speaks affectionately of the pea-shooters he made as a boy. A piece of willow or hazel could be fashioned into a neat weapon with a little patience. Less destructive were the whistle pipes made in a similar way.

Empty tin cans were always in demand. An inventive child could use these to make winter warmers – the tins perforated and filled with smouldering rags. Then there was the thrill of joining two tins with a piece of string, to make a crude telephone. Two pound treacle tins, with two holes in the top and strings threaded through, could become rather basic stilts.

Equally basic were the cardboard whizzers made by cutting out two rings of card, making two holes in the centre of each, and threading thin string through. By pulling and relaxing the string, you could make the disc revolve, producing a satisfactory whizzing sound.

Sometimes adults could be persuaded to share their rather more sophisticated toys, such as the wheel of life, which Mr Goatcher remembered his father bringing out on special occasions. The children of the household were enchanted by the different series of cards used in the toy.

Several older folk have told me about prick books. The books were made up of pictures of any kind, and you turned the pages so that the illustrations were hidden. To have a go you stabbed a pin through the page, and if lucky you reached a picture. If not, you lost your pin. Pity about the pictures though!

When anyone mentions toy boats I immediately think of the beautiful creations which appeared in the summer months on the Oyster Pond at Littlehampton. This was the pool used in earlier days by the fishermen to store their oysters.

Sailing a model yacht in the sea at Bexhill

In my childhood it had been turned into an ornamental pond, for children (and adults) to sail their model yachts. These were hardly toys, more works of art, or so it seemed to me as I watched with envy these beautiful models being carefully lowered into the water by their proud owners.

TREATS

What visions of delight that magic word 'treat' once conjured up in the minds of children a century or so ago. Queen Victoria's Golden Jubilee in 1897 was a very busy year for treats; commemorative mugs, school holidays, sweets and fireworks. Perhaps being a child at that time wasn't too bad, after all.

Mrs Bowyer told me of the treat held in Hurst Park (now Horsham Park). Children marched to Gaol Green (the Carfax) – then still largely grass-covered, where they gave three cheers and sang God Save the Queen. There followed a procession led by a Sussex farm wagon, with the horses decorated with greenery. Up the Causeway the children went, through Middle Street and on to the park, where a giant tea awaited them. There were races, swings, roundabouts and swing boats. The children then scrambled for sweets, and as they left each was presented with an orange, a bun and a bag of toffees. The day ended with a grand bonfire on Gaol Green.

Not far away, Crawley also had its Jubilee Fete on June 9, 1897. Here there were sports, a hat trimming contest (for men), a washing contest (presumably for women), balloon ascents and aunt sallies.

To get to the treats farmers' wagons were often used, although sometimes coal carts were pressed into service. These were supposed to be well cleaned beforehand, but this was not always the case, and some children ended up a little less clean at the end of the day than their mothers expected. Those who went to Sunday school at a mission hall in the Queen Parks area of Brighton were transported on their jubilee treat in three coal carts belonging to Mr Hawkins. On the great day, Mr H polished three sets of harness, scrubbed and washed three carts, blackened the horses' hooves, and then turned up on time at the hall. The teachers brought out some hard wooden forms, which were securely roped to the carts. The children were taken to a large house in Dyke Road called Pennies Field. Here on the lawns they ran races and played games. At four o' clock the tea bell tolled and there were long tables laid out with bread and margarine, cakes and jellies.

One memorable treat in Horsham had tea made in large barrels. All commented on the attractive flavour, and it was only later that someone realised the barrels had been provided by the local brewery.

A postcard from Poynings (1910) reads:

> *You ought to have been with our band of merry children yesterday. We had such a jolly time, with tea and strawberries, and games from five o'clock until eight o'clock in Mrs Prewetts field. About fifty girls and boys.*

WALKING

Walking may often have been a pleasure, but it was also a grim necessity at many times, when there was no other way to get to school, or to other places. Adults and children walked all the time, and probably it helped to keep them healthy – well, most of the time!

At the end of the nineteenth century boys walked from Horsham to Plummers Plain (about four miles) in an hour, starting at 11am, in order to hear the carillon of the church ring *The Blue Bells of Scotland* at noon. It performed twice a day – at twelve and six.

Henry Burstow of Horsham tells us that in 1823 Lad Verrall walked 1,000 miles in twenty days for a wager of £30. He started on Tuesday, November 4, 1823, and finished on the night of the 24th – the old band playing him in at the end. At the end his winnings and gifts totalled £300.

THE FIRST REAL JOB

In the past the first job was often of a short term nature. For many youngsters it was necessary to start earning as soon as possible, so there was little choice. One of the most usual first jobs was as an errand boy, delivering almost any kind of goods by means of a heavy and unwieldy trade bike with a huge metal container over the front wheels.

There was, however, one way out of this dead end, as long as parents were not too anxious to receive a share of one's earnings for several years. Apprenticeship always had its advantages and disadvantages, perhaps equally for both master and servant. In the seventeenth and eighteenth centuries it was closely tied to the poor law system, but even then it furnished a willing lad with a trade for the rest of his life, providing he had a fair employer who honoured his obligations to teach the lad the things he needed to know, and did not take advantage of the situation to provide himself with a cheap form of sweated labour. The apprentice, for his part, had to be prepared to go about his master's business in a conscientious manner, keeping his secrets to himself, and not spending his time in the village pub.

In the nineteenth century a typical indenture for a lad who wished to learn the wheelwrighting trade in all its branches might contain such words as the following: *His master he faithfully shall serve, his secrets keep and his lawful commands gladly do. He shall not commit fornication nor contract matrimony within the said term. He shall not haunt tavern nor playhouse, nor absent himself from his master's service day or night.'*

It all sounds very hard, although the master also had to promise that he would teach and instruct and provide sufficient meat, drink, lodging, tools and all necessaries – except for washing, mending of clothes, medicines or medical attendance in the case of sickness. The apprentice was called upon to work a twelve-hour day with time for meals. No doubt it worked well enough, if both sides were reasonable, but equally it may have brought considerable hardship to the lad if his master were ill-tempered or unjust.

Not all the aggravation came from the employer. The established workers were often equally tough on a green youngster, sending him on fools' errands, such as requests for striped paint, left-handed hammers or a yard of pump water. Some apprenticeship customs still survive to the present day. No doubt the new arrivals are still sent on impossible errands, although perhaps modern youths are a little bit more street-wise than their grandfathers. In some industries, particularly that of printing, the lads were subjected to a custom called

Errand boys employed by Mr Hills the butcher in Brighton

banging-out. For this they were placed in a tin bath, and had poured over them a foul concoction containing anything that the imagination of their mates could think up, such as ink, soup, sawdust, flour, custard, wallpaper paste, and even manure and other unmentionable substances. The lads were expected to take it all in good part and, at the end of the day, to buy their tormenters a round of drinks.

In the 1930s shops were still using a form of apprenticeship for young lads leaving school at fourteen. No doubt they did learn a great deal, not all connected with the trade – but they were also a useful form of inexpensive labour, being expected to cope with almost anything that was required of them.

But these were minor irritations compared with some of the practices earlier in the century. Shop boys were expected to stay at work until late in the evenings, leaving goods outside the shops until after the pubs had closed – just in case anyone should wish to make a purchase on their way home. One man told me how his employer had insisted that all the boots and shoes, displayed outside his shop, should remain there until the last pub customers had disappeared.

In previous centuries country boys had few choices of employment, apart from agriculture with its all-weather back-breaking tasks. George Townsend (in his eighties in the 1960s) told me that when he was only fifteen he was already ploughing with two horses on his own. Often when he was ploughing on the hill towards Ditchling Beacon he did not see another human from the time he left home at 6.30am to when he returned in the late afternoon. He had started work on the farm at eleven years of age, walking about two-and-a-half miles each day to get there. A carter's life was not an easy one, as there were few machines and most of the time was spent walking in heavy

The ox boy, at Falmer, c1910

boots, ploughing and sowing. But as compensation there was the harvesting, when there was usually a drop of home-brewed beer provided.

Even market gardening, which sounds a more attractive form of employment, had its good and bad sides. Mr H Goatcher, then in his eighties, told me in 1979 of how as a young lad his ambition was to travel overnight with a loaded cart bound for Brighton produce market. Leaving at about 5pm, they would reach Shoreham before midnight, and stop at the pub. By the early morning they would be in Brighton, dispose of their produce, and then return home to a full day's work. However, on the way, the man or boy who was not actually driving could lay in the middle of the load and snatch a few hours sleep under the moonlight – always supposing it was not raining. As a lad he thought this was an enchanting way to spend a night.

Bill Wickens and his brother Bob were in their eighties in 1982 when they shared some of their memories of the early days helping their father in the Horsham Vicarage garden. It included a large orchard, flower and vegetable plots, greenhouses, lawns and a tennis court. The boys were expected to help after school, at weekends and in holidays, but no payment was made (or expected) for their labour.

The path up to the house had to be kept free of weeds and the boys tackled this task on their knees with the aid of an old flat-ended dinner knife. The mowing of the lawns was also their responsibility, shared at times by their younger sisters. The mower, a fourteen inch Ransome, had to be pulled along with the help of a thick rope fixed over the body and under the arms. The cutting line had to be absolutely straight, so one boy or girl would walk behind to act as a guide and woe betide anyone who trod on the edges of the lawns, which were kept trimmed with a pair of scissors.

Another job which the brothers remembered with some amusement, was pushing the Vicarage silver up the Causeway in a wheelbarrow, to be placed in the bank while the vicar and his family spent their annual holiday in France.

Just as boys often had to look to agriculture for their first jobs, so girls had little choice other than domestic service. Sometimes the girls had to accept jobs a long way from home, as posts were not always available near at hand. Mrs C Chandler, who was nearly ninety when we spoke in 1980, told me that her mother did not want her to go out to work, but it could not be avoided as her father earned so poorly as a carter. She started work at Sheffield Park when she was fourteen, for three and sixpence a week, plus keep. There were around sixteen employed there, and she began as the lowest of the low – a humble scullery maid. She ended her life with permanently bent toes, due to the constant kneeling in her early days.

One possible way for boys and girls to escape work on the land was to obtain a much-coveted job on the railway system. Mrs W Cousins told me in 1980 how she became an attendant at Brighton Railway Station refreshment room in the 1920s. All the girls lived in a large house close to the station under a housekeeper who was very strict. They had to be in at night by a certain hour, unless prior permission had been obtained for a very special reason. They wore black dresses with white collars, and duty time was four hours on and three off, early turn from 7am to 2pm – late turn from 2pm to 10pm. Her wages at that time were fifteen shillings weekly.

SWEETS, TREATS AND GINGERBREADS

Many older readers will have pleasant memories of miniscule sweet shops, sometimes merely the front room of a cottage, presided over by an elderly lady (why were they always elderly?). There would have been big jars of brightly-coloured sweets and almost certainly a farthing table.

Most children, during the early part of the last century, felt themselves lucky if they had pocket-money of a penny a week. In my own case this was always known as my Saturday Penny, and anything over this was considered great riches, only to be earned with great effort or on very special occasions, such as the visit of a far-flung aunt.

The afore-mentioned farthing table was always in great demand, with the customers taking a very long time over their deliberations for one farthing represented a quarter of the whole week's pocket money. Perhaps included were locust beans – the fruit of the carob tree from the Mediterranean, very sweet tasting and reputed to be the food that John the Baptist lived on in the wilderness (now seen in health food shops). Other sweets familiar at that time were Kalibunkers (like a honeycomb); chewing wax (in different flavours), aniseed balls, sherbet dabs, honey drops, humbugs, liquorice (in strings or strips), pear drops and twisted sticks of barley sugar.

Mr Laker of Three Bridges told me sweet-shop owner Mrs Rapley knew the weight of all her fingers when weighing out his favourites. If you asked for twenty-four aniseed balls for a penny, then you got only twenty-four – even if some were halves.

Treacle toffee was made at the back of the shop and was liable to break your front teeth if not sampled with care. Many kinds of nuts were always popular – monkey nuts, tiger nuts and pig (or peg) nuts – although the latter would be provided free of charge and not sold in the sweet shop. The wise child (usually a boy) dug these up with a penknife, going down about four or so inches. The nut was at the end of a long thin root and was considered a great delicacy, although parents usually discouraged the youngsters from eating them.

In the early thirties the little sweet shop on my particular road installed a strange machine on the counter – inviting young customers to gamble a penny to see what kind of confection they might be fortunate enough to win. All depended what colour ball appeared when certain magical actions were carried out. You always won something, usually a triangular bar of chocolate. However, if luck smiled on you, then a different coloured ball appeared and you were given a larger bar or even a whole box of chocs. Mind you I never knew anyone who actually won the latter, which required a golden ball to appear. But incredibly I once received a silver ball, and danced about with excitement, and was suitably rewarded with a much larger bar than usual. My mother took a poor view of the whole contrivance, feeling that my precious penny should be spent on a chocolate bar made by a well known firm such as Cadbury or Rowntree, rather than on a confection provided by a completely unknown manufacturer. But the gambler in me always won.

So far I have not mentioned gingerbread, an eatable for which Sussex, and in particular Horsham, was always considered famous. The rhyme once current was:

> *The bakers to increase their trade.*
> *Make alphabets in Gingerbread.*
> *That folks might swallow what they read.*
> *Every letter was digested,*
> *Hateful ignorance detested.*

Three kinds of gingerbread were made in Sussex. Hard – rich and brown, made with heavy treacle. Toy – daintier and made with light treacle. Parliament – thin and light with crinkled edges, shaped by cutters (and not made in moulds, as the other kinds). Lilian Candlin of Brighton recalled buying the latter at The Olde Bunne Shop in Pool Valley as a small girl – paying three-halfpence for two pieces. Gilt was sometimes added to these gingerbreads, picturing the Royal Arms, Wellington on horseback, a grandfather clock, the Prince of Wales feathers or just a cat or a cock. Old gingerbread moulds may be seen in Sussex museums, often designed for special occasions such as weddings or christenings.

Various fairs were noted for their particular gingerbreads. Nutley Fair was said to be such a rough event that the stallholders nailed their gingerbreads to their stalls to avoid them being stolen. At Brighton's Toy fair, which was held in Holy Week each year, local fishermen monopolised the stalls, which were made out of old boats. On the stalls were toys, fruit, a peep-show and, naturally, gingerbread.

All the Horsham fairs were noted for gingerbread. There are records of eight Horsham makers – two in East Street, three in West Street and others in Queen Street, London Road, and Brighton Road. The maker in East Street was Richardson, with the name persisting up to more recent times as a jam factory.

The poet Shelley, when nine-years-old, wrote to a friend in July 1803:

> *Tell the bearer not to forget to bring me a Fairing – Gingerbread, sweetmeats, nuts and a pocket book.*

No doubt young Shelley would have been familiar with that often-used phrase 'to take the gilt off the gingerbread'.

Rottingdean School c1914. The card has been annotated to show a boarder's dormitory and other features

GOING AWAY TO SCHOOL

Many children spent much of their young lives away from home in boarding schools. This was often because of the belief that this was the finest kind of education, or because the parents were employed in places abroad, and their offspring needed a permanent educational base in England. This was obviously the current state of play for many parents in Victorian and Edwardian days, when many civil servants were needed abroad to run the vast British Empire.

Boarding schools differed widely. Some (probably most) were fine establishments with high standards. Unfortunately there were a small number where standards were less high, at a time when official approval was rather easier to obtain than in present times.

Some idea of the better kind of boarding schools may be obtained by looking at the advertisements and literature of the well-known seats of learning in the past century. One of these schools is shown on the postcard opposite, which was sent by a pupil to an address in Switzerland in 1914. The handwriting is microscopic, enabling her to get as much information on the card as possible – most of it being concerned with all the exams she was taking, and the probable results. Of interest is the manner in which the young lady has added to the picture, with information on the rooms in the school – including the position of her bed in one of them.

Also in my files is a scrapbook dating from 1911, kept by a young lady who lived in Brighton, and who had evidently joined the pupils at a very imposing school (St

James's, West Malvern) quite a long way from home. There are pictures of the girls in class, and playing hockey. There are lists of all the girls in various forms, and details of an end of term entertainment. In Dormitory 111, we are told:

> *The windows are our constant care.*
> *And Una is not fond of air;*
> *But be the weather wet or fair,*
> *We open them.*

A fancy dress dance caused much excitement about where and how to get suitable dresses, and those who were clothed in paper and cardboard were unable to sit down during the evening. At the end of the event it was difficult to remember from whom the various garments had been borrowed. The beautifully kept scrapbook concludes with pictures of a return to Sussex and some very sedate holiday activities.

PUNCH AND JUDY SHOWS

Some of my most pleasurable memories of seaside holidays in Sussex, were of the Punch and Judy men, and in particular Uncle Charlie at Littlehampton. I feel sure this very patient man must have grown very tired of seeing the intense fair-haired lad who stationed himself near the front of so many of his shows – particularly as when the bottler came around for the expected penny, I would mysteriously have merged into the passing crowd, only to re-appear again when the danger had passed. My allowance when on holiday at that time was a penny a day, and that had to provide me with some refreshment at some time. The show, as I well recall, started as a straight-forward Punch and Judy booth operated by Uncle Charlie. Then he was joined by Uncle Tony and together they presented a complete programme of puppets, conjuring and humour. Other Sussex resorts had their own Punch and Judy favourites – Tom Kemp at Brighton, who was reputed to keep a real crocodile to take part in his show, and Uncle Percy at Hastings. Sometimes London Punch and Judy men were known to spend part of the summer in Brighton.

These patient puppeteers were continuing a long line of entertainers going back to ancient mystery plays. A statuette of Pulcinello, discovered in 1717, was completely recognisable as our Mr Punch, with the long nose, the hunchback and the goggle eyes. Why has this Italian rascal taken such a firm hold on the imagination of children, with his popularity continuing unbroken until the present day? Really we should discourage our youngsters from using such a role model, considering that he includes murder,

Uncle Charlie and Uncle Tony at Littlehampton Common, 1938

Punch and Judy on a Hove beach, 1935

wife beating, and the killing of policemen among his many activities. But then he is so engaging and full of fun that we just have to laugh and allow him to carry on.

The classic tale is of Punch strangling his infant in a fit of jealousy. Punch is rebuked by his long-suffering wife Judy, and adds wife-killing to his other faults. He is caught by the policeman, who meets with the same fate as the wife and baby. An attempt is then made by Jack Ketch to execute him by hanging, but this proves difficult as he is helped by the unexpected appearance of a crocodile. Dog Toby (often a real dog, rather than a puppet) also comes into it, and there is much other basic slapstick humour mixed in at the whim of the operator. Other characters may also make an appearance, such as a doctor, a ghost (very popular this one), a clown, a devil and, we must not forget, the baby. Punch has his own very distinctive voice which is produced by the operator using a kind of whistle, made of two pieces of metal with silk between.

Punch seems to be immortal, and his grotesque form still appears regularly, not only on our seaside beaches, but also, surprisingly, at otherwise highly respectable events such as vicarage tea parties. What is more, present-day children forget their videos and computer toys for a short while, and take this terrible villain completely to their hearts.

A SUSSEX CHILDHOOD IN THE TWENTIES

I was born in a house in two roads. Perhaps I should explain. The small house had been built in the nineteenth century on a narrow piece of ground bounded on both sides by a road. On one side was the front door facing on to a relatively posh terrace, which had once had gates at one end. The other road had the back door, which opened via a gate directly on to a busy road, so that one took a risk every time it was necessary to leave by that exit – and back doors were always used in preference to the front which was reserved for very special occasions. Admittedly most of the traffic was horse drawn, but it still seemed hazardous in those more leisurely times.

Certainly the back door road was the more interesting, as it held such exciting things as a corn merchants yard, a blacksmiths forge, and an inn yard where not so very long before, coach and fours had stopped on their way to the coast. My mother also recalled with affection the flea-pit Cinema Gem which had also occupied a popular site in the road; but sadly this disappeared before my time.

When my parents married, my father was only bringing home boys' money, so cash was very scarce. The only place they could find to live was with my aunt in the house already mentioned. This meant two rooms upstairs, with no running water. The loo was down the garden path. How my poor mother managed a baby in such conditions I have no idea, as it meant a journey downstairs and through my aunt's kitchen and scullery just to obtain a jug of water. Meantime, my father had to depend on work paid by the hour, which meant if no jobs were available, then he was laid off and no money came in. When he was in work it often meant a long cycle ride, whatever the weather, to a building site in the depths of the country, with no pay for the time spent travelling to the job.

But I was too young to worry about such things, being more concerned with the strange men who worked in the corn merchants yard down the road. To protect their heads they wore cowl like headgear fashioned from old sacks, which gave them a medieval monk-like appearance. Rather frightening for a three-year-old, although I must admit they always appeared friendly enough, and there were always the many playful cats and kittens that ran around in the yard, and welcomed the attentions of a small boy. Sometimes my mother took me in to the little shop in the adjacent street kept by the maiden lady who owned the corn and feed business. Here the smell – a mixture of grain, fertiliser and milk chocolate – was completely heavenly. If my mother had a spare penny (which was only occasionally) she would buy me a chocolate bar from the good lady behind the counter. Life was good in those days!

When I was about four years old my parents moved to a flat about a mile from the centre of the town. This was actually only three small rooms on the second floor of a house that had once been a laundry. There was no water laid on in the room which we used as a kitchen, although – heaven – there was an inside toilet.

Close by were several local shops which soon became very familiar. There was the little grocers on the corner, with the wonderful bacon slicing machine. The proprietor employed two young lads who looked very much alike, in fact I never learnt to tell them apart – although my mother said they were not related.

Across the road was the local sweet shop kept by an old couple, although it seemed that the elderly lady did all the work. As well as selling sweets, they ran a lending library with a range of romantic novels much to my mother's taste. Here I would be despatched to fetch the latest in heart-throb stories to break the monotony of Mum's daily life. In a side room the two sons ran a men's barbers shop. This kept very busy and the two brothers appeared to have no interest in the rest of the business. Here I had my curls removed and my first grown-up haircut, much to my satisfaction – particularly when the barber called me by my father's christian name instead of my own.

On yet another corner was Mrs Jackman's bakers shop. This particularly fascinated me as it appeared that anyone could bake a cake and have it cooked in this good lady's oven. I did not much care for egg custards but once when I was ill my mother beguiled me into eating one by insisting that it had been cooked by Mrs Jackman in her very own oven.

Not so far away was Mr Grace's farm, and now that I was a big boy, soon to go to school, I was allowed to go by myself to fetch milk in my mother's white jug. Fine – until I met the farmer's herd of cows returning home from the fields. I was not actually afraid of cows, but I found an urgent reason to disappear into the cover of the hedgerow while they passed by. We received a daily delivery every morning by the farmer, and in addition each afternoon he despatched a neat little milk float drawn by a clever horse around the local roads, so that housewives who had run short could sally forth with their jugs and obtain fresh supplies. In the summer the big churn containing the milk was kept cool (or at least apparently so) by a spotless white cover. The horse knew all the regulars and would stop without being told at every house where a request for milk was likely to appear

My favourite day of the week was Saturday. My father finished work at midday, and later we would set forth to do the main weekly shop in the town. This meant walking to the shops, although I knew that the journey home after dark would be by bus – a great treat. The local bus service was run by a family firm, and most often the little bus was driven by the son of the proprietor, who had a great reputation as a wit. I would hang on his every word, although some of his jokes were a bit beyond my understanding.

The one and only snag to these Saturday outings was the fear that we would see the blind man who sold matches. I am absolutely certain that this poor man was perfectly harmless, and probably a very nice person, but for some unexplained reason he just scared me to bits, and I dreaded even seeing him at a distance. At some point we would visit the little market in the centre of the town, and here I would be absolutely entranced by all the strange people who sold what appeared to be even stranger things. There were those who pulled teeth, tended feet and supplied a number of things which I was not even allowed to see. Then there were the auctions of foodstuffs, and the thrill of warming ourselves by a large open brazier.

At the end of the evening shops sold off their perishable goods at knock-down prices, and this was the time to get real bargains, as my parents knew only too well. Sometimes I visited the town shops on a weekday with my mother, although the fascination of Saturday night was absent.

Before I leave the shops, I must mention Woolworths' Threepenny and Sixpenny Stores. Mind you this was sometimes craftily maintained. For instance, I remember my aunt buying me a camera in Woollies, paying sixpence each for five separate pieces of the camera, to be assembled by the purchaser. But it worked well enough, and I still have some of the tiny snaps to prove it.

Sundays were a mixed blessing. We were a church going family, so this meant the long walk down to the town church twice (and even sometimes three times) in the day. It seemed a long way for my little legs. One Sunday evening my parents apparently thought it was time I was rewarded, and they took me into a little shop on the way home, and bought me an ice cream. But this was an ice cream such as I had never before tasted. Instead of a rather insipid three-cornered bar of flavoured ice, this was soft ice cream served with a wafer in a little saucer, and what is more we sat at a little round table to eat it. A chance to sample how the rich lived!

My rich uncle – at least that was how I thought of him, although I believe he was in fact a company rep – began to visit us by car with my aunt and cousin on Sunday afternoons, taking us out for a picnic in the country. What bliss. I doted on my girl cousin, who was four years older, and liked to mother me, and my aunt was always full of laughter. This definitely perked up Sundays for one little lad.

My grandparents lived at Littlehampton, and occasionally we would visit them by Southern Railway. However, this was also on Sundays, and in honour of the visit I was dressed in my Sunday best, and was not even allowed to sample the slot machines on the seafront. But I loved to see Gran, who although relatively poor was very good to me in every possible way. She instituted what became known as Grannies Parcels. These came up to us by Southdown bus and had to be collected at the bus office in the centre of the town (much cheaper than parcel post). We were alerted to these parcels by a penny postcard arriving the day before, and I could hardly wait until we had collected and carried home the large lumpy parcel which my dear grandmother had managed to make up. Inside would be some particularly tasty broken biscuits which she bought from a Littlehampton shop, and some toy or toys for me. These were always secondhand and had been obtained by Gran from the well-to-do family where she worked as a cleaning lady. But even if well-used, they were always expensive toys, such as I would never have seen otherwise. Gran's parcels were undoubtedly a very bright spot in an otherwise rather humdrum world.

One other amusement for Sundays was in watching the traffic, which increased every year as I grew up. The first traffic lights in Sussex were installed, and soon there was a steady stream of cars heading for the coast, and back in the evening, every weekend. Later a large notice appeared pointing to the coast road, informing passers-by that this was the way to Butlins at Littlehampton – not a holiday camp, but an amusement park which had been built partly over the site of the old Littlehampton windmill. I loved the amusements, but hated to see the old mill disappear.

Christmas was always a very special time. First there would be the making of the puddings, including the ritual stirring and the insertion of several threepenny pieces.

Woolworths once again came into its own, for here I bought most of my presents, having saved up for many weeks beforehand. Most of these, apart from those for my parents, cost the vast sum of threepence. Somehow when I did my present-buying I always seemed to have a few pence over at the end, so I was able to buy one further gift for myself.

Some of the joy of Christmas came in just looking. There was the expensive shop which always filled its main window with equally expensive crackers, and the fishmongers that turned itself into a provider of game birds, which were hung all over the front of the premises, so that the actual shop windows were completely covered.

An important day shortly before Christmas was when my mother took me with her to the Maypole Stores to choose items from her Christmas Club. During the year she had regularly saved sixpence a week, and now was the magic moment to spend all this wonderful cash on such things as dates, mincemeat, crystalised fruits and nuts. What is more I was allowed to have a say in choosing exactly what we would take home. There was also the evening when the Tontine Club had its Christmas share-out. Again this had been saved-for during the preceding year, and the money helped to buy presents for relatives and friends of my parents.

On Christmas Eve we always went to Midnight Mass, something magical which I would not have missed for all the world. I had to go to bed at my normal time, and was then awakened about an hour before midnight, to have a damp flannel rubbed over my face, and then the walk to the church through the cold winter air. Afterwards there was the walk home, with perhaps a pick-a-back from my father for the final distance. And then into bed too sleepy to worry about that huge kitbag with the strange bulges waiting for morning at the bottom of my bed.

On Boxing Day we always visited my great uncle in the country, taking a Southdown bus (which in those days ran even on Boxing Day). Uncle and Aunty, as everyone called them, lived in a house surrounded by a large garden and with such enchanting things as chickens and pigeons close by. The water came from a pump and the whole house smelt of apples and other country aromas. In the afternoon the men (and that included me) went for a walk, with my uncle carrying his gun under his arm. I was allowed to fire it once, although once was enough. Later we sat round playing silly parlour games, and I marvelled at how grown-ups could change just because it was Christmas. Lastly there was catching the bus home in the dark, with my uncle carrying a storm lantern which he used to wave down the double-decker bus when it arrived. What a wonderful day.

A SUSSEX BEDTIME STORY

This yere tale consarns a terrible deep 'ole, at a li'l 'ole place called Lyminster near Lil'hampton. This 'ole were so deep that nuffin and nobody 'ad ever bin known to reach the bottom, and when all the wells in Lyminster wur dry this 'ole allus 'ad water in it.

One day the ole bhoys thought it would be a good notion to tie the ropes offen the Lyminster church bells together, an let 'em down in the 'ole, but 'twas no use – the whole lot of ropes together still didn't reach the bottom, and so they 'ad to give up trying.

One day dunamy years ago a local lad name o' Jim Pulk, wor traipsing around out Lyminster way an he stopped to wet 'is whistle in the Six Bells. Some of the folks there woz a chirping like a Jackdaws' Parliament bout a dratted dragon called the Knucker, wot lived in a gurt big 'ole, jes like a genelman, frittin o' the folks living close-by sumthin tarrible.

Truth to tell, they jest couldn't abear 'im, wot with grabbin all their cows and ship, and even their liddle cats and dogs. Not content wi' that, the varmint kep 'em awake onights, wi' his noisy snufflings and slobberings. Folks who had seed 'im, said 'e wur a terrible big size, shaped partly like a sarpint and partly like a 'ooman, wi' a mortal bad temper. 'E 'ad a pair o' gurt big ole wings on 'is sides, an 'e used 'em to 'nable 'im to swoop down on the ole farmer's beasties, and then carry 'em orf to is 'ole.

Sims as 'ow the locals ad sent a Billy-Douz to the ole King, beggin o' 'im to rid 'em o' the dragon. So the King thort 'e 'ad bettermost offer a middlin big reward to anyone who could kill the beastie. So 'e made up a lil job lot o' jewels and sich, but this turns out to be nohows no use, cos all the local bhoys wur too afeared o' the dragon to get near 'im. So the King 'e 'ad another think and decided 'e 'ad better offer the 'and o' is bootiful li'l darter to the first brave bhoy who would rid Lyminster o' its dragon.

Becus she wuz a rare beauty, an a nice li'l lass as well, this 'elped a few young men to make up their minds to 'ave a go. The fust wuz a knight who popped on 'is armour and tried 'is luck – but that ole dragon grabbed 'im in 'is coils and crushed 'im to a jelly. The next one to try wur a miller who took a pook o' flour wi' 'im to throw in the dragon's eyes to blind 'im. But this didn't work too well either, an' the miller weren't 'eard of again.

The Lyminster folk tole Jim that nobody and nuffin could be dun 'bout it – but Jim wur a valiant sort of kiddie an he thowt he could find someways to get shot of this pesky beastie. 'Get me a gurt sack o' flour, an a middlin lot o' fats and currants, an' a mite o' rat poison, an' we'll see wot we can,' sez li'l ole Jim. So the folks skaddled about and kim up wi' all the 'gradients Jim 'ad asked 'em for. These he mixed up in a mortacious big pot 'til 'e were quite beazled.

Then the pudden woz lifted onto a Sussex cart and carried down to the dragon's 'ole. But Jim 'ad another thowt an' said 'Get me sum sugar, jest to mek the ole thing more tasty-like. 'Twill be jest like the plumb-heavies and swimmers my mother meks.'

When young Jim wer satisfied wid the pudden he called out 'Come out Mr Dragon. I got sumfin' that I rackon you'll like even betterer than cows and ship.' The dragon shuffled out, kinda suspicious like, but when he smelt o' the pudden, he ope'd his gurt big mouth and swallowed the whole lot, pudden, cart, 'orse an all.

Bi'me-by the varmint started to act all squimbly like, as if 'e 'ad the biggest-land an' the worst-rip, complaining that 'e had a mortal gurt belly-ache. 'Sarves you right,' says Jim. 'You jest oughter 'ave behaved yerself bettermost.' 'Fore long the groans died away an' when Jim and the other folks pooked the dragon wi' their dibbers an' 'ooks 'e rolled over and wid one more girt big groan 'e died. Jim, jest to be on the safe-side like, borrowed a chopper and cut off the varmint's 'ed. Then 'e went back ter the Six Bells and tole all 'is other friends jest wot 'ad 'appened. The folks wur so pleased wid 'im that they axed 'im to bide in the village along o' 'em.

Some do say that he stayed an' married the li'l princess when she were old enuff. Corse others said she wur only a dasen't village lass, but p'raps she simmed like a princess to Jim in 'is deedy way.

Now don't let narry-a-one tell 'e that this 'ere tale t'aint true like, 'cos you can still see Jim's tomb in the church, and the gurt big 'ole where the dragon lived is still there today – an' they still haven't got to the bottom of it. So the tale must be true – surelie!

REFERENCES

I have dipped into the riches of several authors while researching this book. These are some of them – for which I am truly grateful.

Beckett, Arthur: *Adventures of a Quiet Man*, 1933
Charman, Aubrey: *Southwater Through 200 Years*, ND
Copper, Bob: *A Song for Every Season*, 1971; *Early to Rise*, 1976
Hall, Doris: *Growing up in Ditchling*, 1985
Hall, Helena: *Lindfield Past and Present*, 1960
Johnson, Steve and Leslie, Kim: *Scholars and Skates*, 1989
Johnson, WH: *Seaside Entertainment in Sussex*, 2001
Longley, A: *Alexandra Terrace*, 1960
Muggeridge, Ron: *Warnham, a History*, 1985
Opie, Iona and Peter: *The Lore and Language of School Children*, 1985
Parish, WD: *A Dictionary of the Sussex Dialect*, 1875/1957
Read, Len: *Slinfold Through 80 Years*, 1988
Ridel, Alfred T: *Ninfield in the Nineties*, 1979
Sargent, Gilbert: *A Sussex Life*, 1988
Stanford, JJ and Muggeridge, RAH: *Warnham, A History of Sports and Pastimes*. 1988
Taylor, Rupert: *The East Sussex Village Book*, 1986
Wolseley,Viscountess: *The Countryman's Log Book*, 1921

I have also perused the pages of the following periodicals, finding much of interest:
Brighton Herald, Petworth Society Magazine, Sussex County Magazine, Sussex Life, Sussex Notes and Queries, West Sussex County Times, West Sussex Gazette, West Grinstead Catholic Magazine.

Many kind folk have helped me write this book, although they will not have realised this when they so willingly offered me their memories. To them, including several no longer with us, I owe a tremendous debt of gratitude for allowing me to draw on their experiences, and in some instances, their photographs. They are:

G Attrill, F Barton, Mr Blunden, Miss L Candlin, E Carley, Mrs C Chandler, RH Charters, B Copper, E Corfield, M Costello, W Cousins, CW Cramp, W Creighton, W Crouch, Miss M Curtis, A Garner, H Goatcher, Mrs H Goddard, Miss D Hall, Mrs I Hill, T Laker, SL Longhurst, Mrs M Lovekey, S McCarthy, Mrs M Moran, R Muggeridge, Mr and Mrs P Nightingale, J Payne, Mrs RMM Piggott, Mrs E Powell, Mrs J Sunderland, Mrs PA Thressel, G Townsend, Mrs E Vincent, W and R Wickens, Mrs MC Willis.

About the author

Tony Wales was born in Horsham in 1924 and has lived there for most of his life. Originally he

worked in the music business, becoming Press and Public Relations Officer of the English Folk Dance and Song Society at its national headquarters, Cecil Sharp House, in London. After nearly twenty years, during which time he compiled many books on folk music, he moved on to become the London manager of the American Library of Congress. After retirement Tony ran his own academic book-selling business for several years. For the last quarter-century he has been writing books on Sussex folklore and old country life. They include – *We Wunt be Druv; A Sussex Garland; Ballads, Bands and Bellringers; Sussex Customs, Curiosities and Country Lore* and *A Treasury of Sussex Folklore.*